AT HOME
WITH PLANTS

AT HOME

Ian Drummond & Kara O'Reilly

WITH PLANTS

STYLING BY ELKIE BROWN
PHOTOGRAPHY BY NICK POPE

MITCHELL BEAZLEY

CONTENTS

THE HOUSEPLANT REVIVAL

There is no doubt that houseplants are once again 'having their moment'. In recent years, gardeners have been surprisingly circumspect when it came to indoor plants. But, with the return of a more eclectic, vibrant, individual approach to interior decorating, it was only a matter of time before the real plants that inspired the botanical fabrics and wallpapers were once again back in the spotlight.

Although houseplants were a popular feature of home decoration during the 1960s and 1970s, they fell out of favour when the minimalist 1990s hit. But today, together with the revival of interest in craft skills, growing-your-own and baking, people are embracing houseplants as another antidote to the increased demands of our tech-preoccupied world.

In order to be a part of the houseplant revival, many of us need to overcome our fear – that sense that we have no idea what to do with them or how to look after them. The good news is that, with a little know-how, even the least green-fingered among us can successfully grow an indoor plant – or two.

As well as being a foolproof guide to caring for houseplants, this book is also intended to be a go-to resource for creative ideas on where to position

WHY REAL, NOT FAUX?

Given that faux plants have come on in leaps and bounds in how much they resemble the real thing and that you can find pretty much any plant you can think of reproduced in fuss-free fakery, why choose the real thing? Because, let's face it, a faux is basically an ornament, whereas living plants change and evolve over time. A thriving plant is part of nature's rich cycle, and no amount of good fakery can replicate that. Bringing a part of nature into your home in the form of plants and nurturing them to give their best is hugely rewarding. What's more, they offer significant health benefits, too – but more of that later.

them and how to display them. Start small with, say, a cactus or a succulent, and once you've proven your plant-caring skills, we guarantee you will want to introduce more into your home.

Ian and I are going to show our ages now, but we distinctly remember the role that plants played in the decoration of our childhood homes. From dramatic, glossy *Monstera deliciosa* (Swiss cheese plant) and *Ficus elastica* 'Decora' (rubber plant) in the living room to macramé-clad hanging *Chlorophytum comosum* (spider plant) in the kitchen, plants were embraced by our parents as decorative objects. With the advent of the yuppie 1980s, we, too, had the ubiquitous *Yucca elephantipes* (spineless yucca) in our teenage bedrooms. Like many others before us, we grew herbs in pots in the kitchen and bulbs in window boxes in our first apartments. For me, this segued into the cactus years and the odd purchase from East London's Columbia Road

flower market – I still feel sad about the beautiful *Ficus benjamina* (weeping fig) that didn't survive when I moved apartments. Ian, meanwhile, had the benefit of being able to bring home plant samples from work and became particularly fond of his *Spathiphyllum wallisii* (peace lily).

We have both observed the creeping return of greenery in the way some of the chicest folk around decorate their homes today. We have noticed cool interiors companies upping the variety of plant pots in their ranges, and the resurgence of both terrariums and hanging planters as decorative elements in the design of cutting-edge boutique restaurants, shops and cafés.

Now is the time to embrace this trend and run with it in your own home. With Ian's expertise to hand, we are hoping to help you break out of the safe zone of a supermarket basil plant that will wilt away like an afterthought in your kitchen. We hope to inspire, inform and help you innovate with the way you use plants in your home. One of the most amazing things about houseplants is that you can enjoy them all year round, and there is really nothing more satisfying to the soul than nurturing a living thing.

Left:
This open terrarium is filled with a selection of small succulents and finished with some *Cladonia rangiferina* (reindeer moss), which is a type of lichen.

Above:
A collection of hardy succulents, cacti and two bold *Sansevieria* – *S. bacularis* 'Mikado' and *S. cylindrica* – complement the dark wood of this modern sideboard.

TRENDS & AESTHETICS

The re-emergence of the houseplant as a key feature in so many interior schemes has seriously gathered momentum over the last year or two. And the keen-eyed will have observed that the predominant design choice is evergreen plants.

Cacti and succulents are back in vogue, which can be put down to the popularity of terrariums as the preferred plant container among the cognoscenti. However, dramatic, large-scaled plants, such as those 1970s favourites *Monstera deliciosa* (Swiss cheese plant), ferns and *Fatsia japonica* (Japanese aralia), are also having their moment once again in the spotlight. Their aesthetic appeal in an interior lies in their bold shapes and the impact that these can have. You just have to look at how top interiors companies such as House of Hackney or Cole & Son have used plants like these as the pattern inspiration for some of the coolest wallpaper and fabric prints around.

We can put all this down to the anti-minimalist backlash. After the pared-back, all-white, clean-line years, we have worked out that our homes are

BACK IN VOGUE

Once consigned to the style compost heap, the following stalwarts of 1970s houseplant schemes are seriously back in favour. They are all evergreen, with striking silhouettes and interesting leaf shapes, which means that they will have an instant impact on an interior.

* *Aspidistra elatior* (cast-iron plant)
* *Asplenium nidus* (bird's nest fern)
* *Chlorophytum comosum* (spider plant)
* *Fatsia japonica* (Japanese aralia)
* *Ficus elastic* 'Decora' (rubber plant)
* *Monstera deliciosa* (Swiss cheese plant)
* *Sansevieria trifasciata* (mother-in-law's tongue)

actually our sanctuaries, not display homes in a real-estate agent's brochure. Using colour, pattern and accent accessories is all about creating spaces that are truly personal to us. Plants fit well into this decorative approach, and if you look at them as pieces of living art that bring extra layers of interest to your home, it becomes easier to know which ones to choose and where to put them.

Many of us also live in increasingly urbanized environments, with little or no access to outside space, so introducing houseplants into your home is the perfect way of reconnecting with nature. You could even do as Ian does and treat them as members of the family – he goes so far as to give some of his particular favourites names…

Technological advances made in the way professional nurseries now propagate and grow plants mean that they are much more affordable than they were, say, a decade ago. Nurseries in the Netherlands can produce literally millions of one variety of orchid, which makes the cost per plant around a quarter of what it was when orchids first emerged as a popular indoor plant a few years ago.

Affordable plants, combined with the easy availability of cool containers in stores and online, as well as simple yet inspirational ideas from the likes of Pinterest, Instagram or the interiors of fashionable restaurants and shops, mean we can all attempt a planting scheme that suits our taste, our space and our creative side.

> **TIP**
> ....
> Stuck for a hostess gift? *Cyclamen persicum*, *Jasminum polyanthum*, *Capsicum annuum*, *Echeveria secunda* var. *glauca* and *Sempervivum tectorum* will all last longer than a bottle of wine.

THE NEXT BIG THING?

Following on from the hippy-chic good looks of knotted, woven and macramé plant holders, *kokedama* is the latest creative way of displaying houseplants – without containers.

Kokedama, which translates as 'moss ball', has its origins in Japan, where it is an offshoot of traditional bonsai (the art of deliberately stunting the growth of a tree or shrub for ornamental reasons), and it is already making its influence felt everywhere in the world of design and display. It involves removing a plant from its pot, shaking off the potting compost, then wrapping the root system in a kind of mud ball (made from a very particular mix of compost and specialist minerals and clays), before covering it with a layer of living moss tied in place with string.

Eye-catching? Definitely. High maintenance? Yes, indeed. So, if it all sounds like too much hard work, you can always use a *Vanda* orchid, *Platycerium bifurcatum* (staghorn fern) or a few *Tillandsia* (air plant) instead to achieve the dramatic effect of a plant suspended in space.

Left:
Succulents, such as this *Echeveria*, are particularly appealing due to their architectural shape and interesting leaf colours, as well as their indestructible qualities.

Above right:
That 1970s staple, the *Chlorophytum comosum* (spider plant), is back in a big way. Display it in a macramé or hanging planter for a nod to retro chic. It thrives in bathrooms and kitchens.

These colourful olive-storage tins at Rockett St George lend themselves to some kitchen planting

Roots glass plant pot by Istanbul-based design company, Nude Living

Succulents on show at hip hairdressers 4th Floor

Danish interior design company Madam Stoltz accessorizes with some dramatic planting (at Out There Interiors)

Hanging planters by Danish brand Bloomingville (at Out There Interiors)

Christian Lacroix's plant-inspired Soft Jardin Exo'Chic fabric for Designers Guild

Palm Jungle wallpaper from the Contemporary Restyled collection by Cole & Son

A cupboard planting scheme by Danish company Nordal (at Out There Interiors)

The Tarovine wallpaper and fabric print by House of Hackney

A collection of cacti styled by design team Darkroom

The restaurant Rawduck showcases a bold line-up of indoor plants

Tiny terrariums by hip homeware e-tailers Rockett St George

Glass herb vases by Cox & Cox

The Paint by Conran look book features plenty of planting

A *Monstera deliciosa* (Swiss cheese plant) accessorizes the Habitat look book

A collection of differently shaped terrariums at interiors emporium Graham & Green

This linen cushion features the iconic Palmeral print by House of Hackney

Contemporary ceramic hanging planters by e-boutique MiaFleur

THE PRACTICALITIES

HEALTH BENEFITS

You know that sense of wellbeing you get in spring when you walk by all the fresh, vibrant greens of new growth in parks and gardens and on trees in the street? With a couple of houseplants, you can experience that feeling all year round.

Connecting with nature and the natural world is just plain good for the soul. Given the fact that so many of us now spend more time indoors than ever before, chained to our laptops, it stands to reason that bringing some of the great outdoors into our interior spaces will have a positive effect on our sense of wellbeing. This is particularly relevant if you don't have immediate access to, or even a good view of, a garden or any green outdoor space.

There have been numerous studies into the health benefits of having plants in the workplace, so you can bet your bottom dollar they will have a positive effect in your home as well. Plants are, after all, the Earth's oxygenators. The by-product of photosynthesis is oxygen, and there can be no harm in introducing a couple of natural oxygenators to your home environment.

While more specific research into the exact environmental and health benefits of each plant variety still needs to be done, many initial studies – undertaken by bodies as varied as NASA and a number of universities worldwide – have come to the conclusion that plants act as a kind of 'pollutant sponge'. This means they absorb all kinds of nasties in the atmosphere, from carbon dioxide to the various volatile organic compounds (VOCs) released from many common man-made products, including paint, carpets, furniture and cleaning products. Plants are able to remove these toxins from the air through their leaves and stems, or through their roots via the potting compost, where small microbes turn the toxins into food for the plant. It's a win-win situation.

These VOCs are believed to be responsible for SBS (Sick Building Syndrome), that affliction of the modern-day office (see also page 137). Those affected can experience headaches, dizziness, fatigue, irritation of the skin, eyes, nose and throat, and more serious ailments such as asthma.

Plants are good for your mental wellbeing, too; looking after and responding to something living is therapeutic. Again, work-focused studies have shown that having plants around can help reduce feelings of negativity, anxiety, depression and stress. No one particular plant does this job better than any other, so to benefit from the positive psychological effects, choose a plant that you really like or feel connected to. It stands to reason that it will make you happy every time you look at it. Put simply, growing green things is good for your health as well as your home.

This page:
Plants are nature's oxygenators, so will improve the air quality in your home. Groupings, such as this *Beaucarnea recurvata* (elephant's foot), *Philodendron scandens* (heart-leaf philodendron) and a selection of ferns, will have more impact health-wise than a single plant.

This page:
This display of easy-to-
care-for indoor plants
includes *Philodendron scandens*
(heart-leaf philodendron),
Anigozanthos (kangaroo paw),
various cacti, *Sansevieria
cylindrica*, *Aglaonema modestum*
(Chinese evergreen),
Beaucarnea recurvata
(elephant's foot), some
Echeveria and *Dracaena*.

CLEANING THE AIR

According to NASA, plants are nature's life support system. The seminal Clean Air Study that it undertook in the late 1980s found that the following plants were among the most effective at filtering toxins and pollutants from the air.

* *Aglaonema modestum* (Chinese evergreen). A lush-leaved, tough plant that can cope with drying out. Ideally needs medium light but can cope with shade. Add some colour by choosing a variety that has patterned foliage.

* *Anthurium scherzerianum* (flamingo flower). Another tough plant that can take a knock, tolerate a bit of neglect and offer more or less continuous colour. Needs medium light.

* *Chlorophytum comosum* (spider plant). As long as it gets a decent amount of light, this plant will pretty much look after itself.

* *Dracaena fragrans* 'Janet Craig' (corn plant). Really hardy, can take low light and will tolerate drying out. Also stays compact.

* *Epipremnum aureum* (devil's ivy). Needs bright to medium light, but can tolerate drying out. A really great trailing plant.

* *Ficus benjamina* (weeping fig). Very good at processing toxins. Will thrive if well looked after: give it a bright spot and leave it well be, as it hates being moved, and don't let it dry out. Other members of the *Ficus* family, such as *F. lyrata* (fiddle-leaf fig) and *F. elastica* (rubber plant), are also good air filters.

* *Phalaenopsis* (moth orchid). Pretty, affordable, easily available and about the toughest orchid out there. Give it a fairly bright spot and remember to soak the roots weekly or mist them daily.

* *Sansevieria trifasciata* (mother-in-law's tongue). As tough as old boots! Able to cope with dark corners and can be left to dry out between waterings. One of the few plants that gives off oxygen at night.

* *Spathiphyllum wallisii* (peace lily). A compact, hardy plant with lush leaves and a beautiful white flower. If it is left to dry out, it will usually recover with a good watering. Needs medium light. Sits well on a desk.

* *Zamioculcas zamiifolia* (fern arum). Particularly adaptable plant that tolerates both bright light and shade. Allow the compost to dry out between waterings.

HOUSEPLANTS & ALLERGIES

* According to the NHS (National Health Service), one in five people in the UK suffers from hay fever. However, the good news is that houseplants, which release few, if any, pollen spores, don't generally bring on bouts of hay fever. However, if you are a sufferer, you are likely to have other allergies as well. In that case, avoid *Ficus* plants, particularly *F. benjamina* (weeping fig), because they exude a latex-like substance on their leaves that can trigger skin allergies.

* Some people think that growing houseplants can actually be a good thing for those with allergies, since plants act as natural detoxifiers, removing pollutants and pollen spores from the air. They also act as filters, causing tiny dust particles to be deposited on their leaf surfaces.

* Remember to clean your plants regularly to avoid any build-up of allergy-causing dust, and make sure you don't over-water, which can result in mould developing on the potting compost and plants, again leading to potential allergic reactions.

PLANT FAMILIES

BOLD

If you want to introduce just one plant into your home but also create the greatest impact with it, then you need to look to architectural plants. Usually the tallest varieties of houseplants available and with dramatic leaves, they are real talking points. Since they are so striking, they work well when displayed singly, as a focal point, rather than in a fussy group scheme. They should be positioned in such a way that their bold silhouettes are seen at their best – in an alcove or a corner that neatly frames them or against a blank wall, for example – which means that they lend themselves to the larger spaces in our homes, such as the living room, dining area or even a generously sized bathroom or kitchen.

Uplighting the plant at night – similar to how a sculpture would be lit in a museum or gallery – is a pleasing touch. After all, such plants are, essentially, living sculptures, and if you think of them in this way, it will also help you decide where and how you might want to display them. Bear this in mind when you look to buy one of these plants. Because of their size, they are investment pieces, so don't start your house-planting career with one of them unless you feel confident that you will be able to care for it properly.

Among the plants that fall into this architectural category are tall foliage plants such as *Ficus benjamina* (weeping fig) and *F. benghalensis* (Indian fig); sculptural-leaved varieties such as *Philodendron bipinnatifidum* (horsehead philodendron) and *Fatsia japonica* (Japanese aralia); palms, like *Dypsis lutescens* (bamboo palm), and false palms, such as *Dracaena fragrans* 'Massangeana' (corn plant); larger ferns like *Nephrolepis exaltata* (sword fern); and large-leaved climbers such as *Philodendron hastatum* (elephant's ear philodendron).

Above:
Euphorbia tirucalli (finger tree) takes several years to reach this kind of size and you would have to order it in especially from a nursery or garden centre.

Right:
One of the most popular indoor palms, *Howea forsteriana* (Kentia palm) is very handsome, as well as extremely low-maintenance.

TIP
....
False palms, so-called because their leaf growth resembles that of a palm tree, make attractive, stand-alone feature plants. Included in this group of common larger houseplants is *Yucca elephantipes* (spineless yucca), *Beaucarnea recurvata* (elephant's foot) and *Pandanus baptistii* (screw pine).

FIVE STATEMENT PLANTS

* *Cycas revoluta* (Japanese sago palm). With its thick trunk and stiff fronds, this exotic-looking plant takes the same form as a palm tree, although it is not actually related to the palm family. Very slow-growing, with a leaf spread of 1m (3ft), it will eventually – after 50–100 years – reach a height of 6m (20ft). Position in bright, but indirect, light, away from radiators. Water frequently in the summer, and sparingly in the winter.

* *Euphorbia tirucalli* (finger tree). This attractive, unusual plant will grow up to 1.5m (5ft) tall, but have a spread of just 50cm (20in), making it particularly suited to small or busy rooms. Its striking new growth has a pink tinge. It needs very little care, just watering every two to three weeks in summer, but requires high levels of light.

* *Phoenix canariensis* (Canary date palm). A classic-looking palm that is very easy to grow, requiring just bright, indirect light and moderate watering. It can grow up to 2m (6½ft) tall, with a spread of 1.5m (5ft).

* *Trachycarpus fortunei* (Chinese windmill palm). This decorative fan palm, so-called because of the shape of its leaves, has a wide spread (2–2.5m/6½–8ft), which makes it suited to larger spaces such as a living room or conservatory. It is slow-growing, highly adaptable and flourishes in bright light. Water regularly.

* *Yucca rostrata*. A tree-like yucca with bluish-tinged leaves that looks great in a living room. It's easy to grow and maintain, but needs bright light. Allow the top of the potting compost to dry out between waterings and feed every two weeks during the growing season. This plant can become top-heavy, so you must rotate it regularly for even growth. It can grow up to 4.5m (15ft) tall and 1m (3ft) wide.

EDIBLE

If you're unable to grow crops outdoors, why not create a bit of a kitchen garden actually inside your kitchen? After all, there's nothing quite so rewarding as growing your own fresh food. As well as looking good, these crops in their containers also mean that you will always have a few essential cooking ingredients to hand.

The idea of growing-your-own is for most people a rather romantic idea, but if you're planning to do so indoors, you must be realistic about what is actually possible. The edible plants that work best in a domestic setting are the smaller kinds, such as herbs, a dwarf citrus, baby salad leaves or the smaller varieties of tomatoes, such as cherry or baby plum. Start off with plug plants if you can, as they will give you bit of a head start.

Once you've succeeded with easier crops such as herbs, and you like the idea of expanding your repertoire, why not try the likes of carrots, radishes, potatoes and the dwarf varieties of beans? However, do bear in mind that all these plants will take up more room than the more obvious indoor edibles suggested on the right.

One other thing worth considering is that edible plants needn't be confined to the kitchen – as long as they receive plenty of bright light, they can also be welcome additions in other parts of the house, such as a dining room or conservatory.

TIP

Edible crops are best grown in glazed ceramic or plastic planters, with plenty of drainage at the bottom. They won't dry out as quickly as terracotta pots.

FIVE EASY INDOOR CROPS

* *Capsicum annuum* var. *annuum* Grossum Group (sweet/bell pepper). Enjoys bright, indirect sunlight and should be watered liberally in spring and summer, but less in winter. Peppers look good planted in terracotta pots and grouped on shelves.
* *Capsicum annuum* (chilli pepper). Grows as small, shrub-like bushes, with fruits in a range of vivid greens, reds, yellows and oranges (a green chilli is an unripe red one). Highly decorative, they make satisfying indoor plants. They need a warm, bright window ledge and moist compost, but do not over-water.
* Herbs need a bright, sunny spot, such as the windowsill. Keep the compost moist, but don't be tempted to over-water. *Allium schoenoprasum* (chives), *Coriandrum sativum* (coriander/cilantro), *Mentha* (mint) and *Ocimum basilicum* (basil) are all worth growing indoors, as are *Artemisia dracunculus* (tarragon), *Origanum majorana* (marjoram), *O. vulgare* (oregano) and *Salvia officinalis* (sage).
* Salad leaves come in all shapes and colours, from the classic *Lactuca sativa* (lettuce) to bitter *Cichorium endivia* (endive), peppery *Eruca sativa* (rocket/arugula), to pretty *Valerianella locusta* (lamb's lettuce). Different varieties planted together look brilliant – try packets of mixed seeds – as well as in juxtaposition with other more ornamental plants, such as *Zamioculcas zamiifolia* (fern arum) and *Aloe variegata* (partridge breast aloe). They need plenty of bright light, so a sunny window ledge is ideal. Keep well watered.
* *Solanum lycopersicum* (tomato). Incredibly easy to grow in the right conditions, bearing abundant fruit in summer and into early autumn. They require very similar care to the *Capsicum* and should be grown in a warm, bright spot. Feed weekly with a tomato feed.

FLOWERS & FRAGRANCE

Smell is probably the most evocative of our senses – the faintest whiff of something familiar can transport you back to a different time or place.

Introducing scented plants into an arrangement of houseplants can also create an additional layer of interest. The same can be said of flowering plants. While the majority of plants that do well in our homes tend to be foliage varieties, there are some flowering plants that can also adapt to the growing conditions indoors. They are more delicate than either hardy or architectural houseplants, so if you plan to invest in some, you will also need to give them the love and attention they need.

Make sure you don't waste a plant's particular scent by clashing it with another perfumed variety. In the confines of a room, one type of perfumed plant is usually enough and often more is more – think about how a mass of *Hyacinthus* (hyacinths) will have a much more pronounced perfume than a single bulb.

The various greens of foliage plants have a neutral hue that tends to fit easily into any room's decorating scheme. While it's not a deal-breaker, it's worth being aware of the depth and shade of the colour of any flowering plants you hope to introduce into a space to make sure that they fit in with the overall look.

TIP

Scent is not confined to flowering plants; many edible plants also give off a lovely fragrance – just think of herbs such as mint, basil and lemon thyme.

FIVE FABULOUS FRAGRANT PLANTS

✽ *Citrus*. Easy-to-obtain citrus plants such as *Citrus* x *microcarpa* (calamondin orange) and the less common *Citrus* x *limon* (otaheite orange) provide a wonderful Mediterranean scent and (small) fruits. Great in kitchens and dining areas, particularly when displayed alone. Place in a bright position; rotate to ensure even growth. Allow to dry out between waterings. Keep out of cold draughts.

✽ *Gardenia jasminoides* (Cape jasmine). These plants are high maintenance but worth the effort for their fragrance. The contrast between the dark green leaves and the white flowers is stunning. Ideal bathroom plants – they love humidity – position near a sunny window, as they need bright, indirect light. Never let the compost dry out completely, but be careful not to over-water. Mist daily.

✽ *Jasminum* (jasmine). Pink *Jasminum polyanthum* (many-flowered jasmine), which is the most usual and easiest variety to grow indoors, is spring-flowering; white *J. officinale* (poet's jasmine) flowers from summer into autumn. Position by a bright window and keep the compost moist. Daily misting will help maintain the pretty blooms. The climbing stems will need support.

✽ *Oncidium* orchids. The small, bright, (usually) yellow flowers make for a cheerful, springtime display and look wonderful en masse in bathrooms and bedrooms. They prefer filtered light – think frosted glass. Allow to dry out between waterings.

✽ *Stephanotis floribunda* (wax flower). The glossy leaves and white, fragrant flowers work well in groupings. Ideal to fill a bedroom with scent. Water frequently in summer; sparingly in winter. Mist daily to prevent the buds from dropping. The climbing stems will need support.

FIVE FANTASTIC FLOWERING PLANTS

* *Aechmea fasciata* (urn plant). Technically speaking, this is not a flowering plant. The striking, bright pink 'flower' is actually a set of leaves on a stalk growing out of the centre of the lower rosette of leathery leaves. This 'urn', designed to collect water, should have water in it all times, but it is important that plants are never waterlogged. They prefer bright, indirect sunlight and are well suited to window ledges. Their bold, tropical appearance makes them a colourful addition to a planting scheme.

* *Medinilla magnifica* (rose grape). These dramatic plants bear spectacular, drooping, rose-pink flowers, provided they are kept in as humid an atmosphere as possible – which makes them perfect for bathrooms. You will need to mist them constantly in spring and summer to encourage and maintain the flowers. They can grow to over 1m (3ft) in height and spread, making them most effective as stand-alone feature plants.

* *Streptocarpus* (Cape primrose). This is now one of the most popular flowering houseplants. Relatively easy to care for, they come in a variety of colours, with blue-purple being the most common, and will flower throughout the summer. They like bright, filtered, indirect light and need to be watered regularly. Useful plants for adding a splash of colour to a landscape grouping.

* *Vanda* orchids. These unusual and versatile orchids come in a variety of colours, but the most striking is a rich, deep blue. Plants will live happily without potting compost as long as the roots are misted every day or submerged in water for an hour once a week. They look most effective displayed en masse, so hang them at different heights to create a living screen or curtain.

* *Vriesia splendens* (flaming sword). The dramatic flowers can grow well over 1m (3ft) tall, but have a narrow spread. Like *Aechmea fasciata* (see left), they are a bromeliad and so the leaves form a natural vase that needs to be kept topped up with water. As long as this 'vase' is filled, you won't need to water the compost unless it dries out. These plants like bright, indirect sunlight and look great on their own due to their strikingly striped leaves and overall form.

> **TIP**
> ....
> Many of the prettiest flowering bulbs, such as *Muscari* (grape hyacinth) and *Convallaria majalis* (lily-of-the-valley), also emit a delicious perfume.

THE CASE FOR CUT FLOWERS?

We can all agree that a flower is a thing of beauty and that every space is brightened up with the addition of a bunch or two. But if you are weighing up the benefits of regularly buying flowers against investing in a flowering houseplant – or two – consider this. Most houseplants sold in Europe are grown in big greenhouses in the Netherlands and, due to their longevity, are transported to their destinations overland. Mixed bouquets of cut flowers, on the other hand, have a shorter life span and may clock up a lot of air miles being transported from their different countries of origin. In the US, although California is the main producer of cut flowers, many still travel long distances from South America. So not only do flowering houseplants give a display that lasts and lasts, they also score points on the eco front as well.

This page:
Grouping together a
collection of the same
family of plants, such as
these *Cattleya*, *Phalaenopsis*
and *Dendrobium* orchids, is
one of the easiest ways of
developing a display.

This page:
Slow-growing *Aglaonema modestum* (Chinese evergreen) can tolerate lower light levels than many houseplants, which makes it particularly versatile.

TOUGH & TOLERANT

These are the kinds of plants to choose if you have never grown houseplants before, or are nervous that you aren't especially green-fingered. Happy to be neglected and best kept on the dry side, they are suitable in most locations in the home. They are also highly adaptable, and many of them can survive in lower light levels. They usually stay pretty compact and work well when arranged in group planting schemes, either in repetition or mixed up as landscapes.

If you're at all unsure about what to buy when shopping for tough and tolerant plants, look out particularly for succulents and cacti. There are now hundreds of varieties of both types of plant available and they are all fairly indestructible. Using succulents as your guide is a pretty good safeguard: other plants with similarly thick and fleshy foliage are likely to be self-sustaining, as succulents are, storing water in their leaves – think along the lines of *Kalanchoe blossfeldiana* (flaming Katy) and *Sansevieria trifasciata* (mother-in-law's tongue).

TIP
....
Getting water on the leaves of succulents or on cacti will damage them, so water by standing plants in a saucer and letting them suck up the water they need until the top layer of potting compost is moist.

TOP THREE SUCCULENTS

* *Crassula ovata* (money tree). Also known as the 'money plant', these exotic hardies require good light and little water. They have beautifully plump, glossy green leaves that are tinged with red, and they retain a bush-like appearance. They're fun, low-maintenance plants, ideal for children's bedrooms, and they look good as part of a shelfie arrangement.
* *Kalanchoe tomentosa* (panda plant). The green leaves are covered with small silver hairs, giving this plant a blue-grey appearance. It should be placed by a bright window. Be careful not to over-water, and do cut off dead flower stems and pinch back leggy growth to keep plants looking their best.
* *Sempervivum tectorum* (common houseleek). This succulent is sometimes called 'hens and chicks' because it produces 'chicks' – miniature plants that are offset from the mother 'hen'. There are many varieties available and all of them seem to thrive on neglect. They work really well planted up as part of a 'living wall' design (see page 59).

SUCCULENT SURVIVAL TIPS

Although succulents are generally tough houseplants, they do make a few demands.
* Succulents prefer bright, natural light.
* They need to be watered generously during the summer months, when their fleshy leaves grow plumper with all the water stored in them.
* Allow them to dry out between waterings because they hate being waterlogged.
* Succulents are more tolerant of the cold than you might expect. This is because they originate from desert regions, where the temperatures drop very low at night.

TOP FIVE TOLERANT PLANTS

* *Aglaonema* (Chinese evergreen). The 21 species of *Aglaonema* all have attractive, oval-shaped leaves growing from a stalk in a variety of leaf colours, many of them with pretty variegated white markings. All of them need moderate watering, and while the all-green varieties, such as *A. modestum*, don't mind lower light levels, the variegated ones, like the silvery-grey *A.* 'Silver Queen', need brighter light, though not direct sunlight. They are slow-growing and look particularly good when grouped together.

* Cactus plants. These come in a wide variety of shapes and sizes, and many flower in the spring and summer. Most are desert plants and so require very little water and virtually no care. Most cacti enjoy bright sunlight and can be displayed in well-lit rooms and on window ledges. It's important to keep the compost well drained and not to over-water. They look great in clusters, grouped on shelves and surfaces. Some cacti can grow to several metres tall and look striking as single plants in heavy terracotta pots.

* *Dracaena fragrans* (corn plant). These plants need good light levels, but they should be kept out of direct sunlight. You only need to water them moderately, and reduce this in winter. Any pruning should be done in spring. They can reach 2m (6½ft) tall but their spread is fairly compact, which makes them ideal for corners and tight spaces.

* *Epipremnum aureum* (devil's ivy). These plants require little care and only average light levels, out of direct sunlight. Their attractive leaves make them particularly striking in hanging and trailing schemes, such as along a shelf edge or in a hanging planter. Prune plants in spring to prevent them from becoming stringy over time.

* *Spathiphyllum wallisii* (peace lily). Of all the flowering houseplants, the peace lily is perhaps the easiest to care for. They prefer bright, indirect sunlight, but can tolerate lower light levels. However, for the plants to bloom, they do require brighter light. The attractive white flowers appear in early summer and can last for weeks.

This page: This table-top display of tough and tolerant plants includes *Ficus pumila* (creeping fig) in the gold bowl; a grouping of *Echeveria* in the zinc pot; and a mature *Beaucarnea recurvata* (elephant's foot) by the window.

TIP
....
Cacti are often thought of as being a separate group of plants, but all of them are, in fact, succulents.

This page:
The various *Echeveria agavoides*
(moulded wax), such as this
'Taurus', are one of the most
widely available and popular
succulents for use indoors.

THE INDESTRUCTIBLES

The following ten plants positively thrive on neglect and, provided that you put them near a natural light source and water them occasionally, they should fight off your best efforts to send them to the big conservatory in the sky. Most of them can, in fact, go without water for up to a month. They can also deal with changes in temperature, as well as tolerate draughts.

TOP TEN (VIRTUALLY) INDESTRUCTABLE PLANTS

* *Aloe.* While these succulents need bright light, they can be allowed to dry out between waterings. They also grow slowly, so you won't have to keep repotting them.
* *Aspidistra elatior* (cast-iron plant). These obliging plants can take a lot of abuse. They have tough leaves that don't mind draughts, changes in temperature and darker locations. They also don't mind drying out between waterings.
* *Chlorophytum comosum* (spider plant). As long as you give spider plants reasonable levels of light, you can then pretty much forget about them.
* *Echeveria.* As with aloes, these succulents require bright light, but they can be left to dry out between waterings. They are also slow growers, so there is no need to repot them.
* *Fatsia japonica* (Japanese aralia). These tough-leaved plants can withstand children and large pets brushing by them roughly, and can also deal with changes in temperature and draughts. Although they don't mind drying out a little between waterings, they do need a decent amount of light.
* *Ficus elastica* 'Decora' (rubber plant). This particular *Ficus* is much better at dealing with reduced light than its cousins. Plants can also be allowed to dry out between waterings.
* *Howea forsteriana* (Kentia palm). Another tough-leaved plant that doesn't mind being around children and large pets. It can also take reduced light levels.
* *Sansevieria trifasciata* (mother-in-law's tongue). These really robust plants can take darker spots in the house, don't mind drying out between waterings and also remain compact, which makes them ideal for hallways.
* *Tradescantia* (wandering Jew). These trailing plants can cope with neglect as long as they are in a reasonably light spot. They look good allowed to grow wild but can also be pruned quite hard.
* *Zamioculcas zamiifolia* (fern arum). These compact plants are happy to dry out and can take a dark location.

CONTAINERS

POTENTIAL PLANTERS

If you put your mind to it, you can use pretty much anything as a container for an indoor plant. The containers you choose depend on the look of your home and the overall effect you wish to achieve. Over-the-top, mix-and-match vintage pitchers, cups and teapots can look just as striking as slick, modern, geometric containers – it's all about context. Take into account the shape, scale and look of the actual plant you are potting up, too – a *Howea forsteriana* (Kentia palm), for example, naturally lends itself to a complementary woven raffia basket, but can look just as fabulous in a contrasting square metallic planter.

But before you go all out on the creative front, you need to check that your chosen container is large enough for the root ball of your plant and that it is waterproof. Also, be aware of the weight and size of the container.

Ian is very experimental when it comes to planters. He will attach air plants to old bottle corks or light bulbs before hanging them in his hallway or kitchen, or create a miniature indoor garden in an old tin bath, sink or vintage suitcase. He has been known to landscape his fire grate for the summer. Once you start looking at every vessel as a potential planter, you'll be surprised at how inventive you can be.

POTTING HOUSEPLANTS

* It's always best to plant directly into your chosen container, having taken the plant out of the plastic pot it came in.
* If your container isn't waterproof, add a liner by painting the inside with either waterproof sealant or pond liner paint. Alternatively, use some thick, industrial plastic sheeting – again, think of the pond lining variety – to create a lining 'bag'.
* Add drainage, such as gravel, small stones or broken-up old terracotta pots, to the base of the container. Aim for a depth of about one-fifth of the overall volume of the pot.
* Follow this with a layer of general-purpose potting compost. How thick this should be will depend on the size of the pot and the plant's root ball – for example, a small root ball in a tall pot will need to sit on a thick base of compost to get it to the right height.
* Position the plant(s) in the pot – in the centre if there's only one – and slowly add more compost, firming it down as you go.
* Water in the plant. If it's a plant that prefers dry conditions, don't go overboard.
* Add some surface dressing, if desired, such as a layer of moss to give the planting a professional finish and help the plants retain moisture (see right).

Left:
Containers for indoor planting schemes come in all shapes, sizes and materials. Simply choose those that suit your particular style and will achieve the desired look.

* Ideally, repot plants at the start of every spring, especially if you are only going up one pot size, i.e., to one that is slightly bigger than the root ball. Add some fresh potting compost and a little plant feed. If you have several plants in a pot and wish to thin them out, this is the time to do it.
* Keeping your plants in small containers can slow down growth but to ensure they stay healthy, keep them in the same pot for a maximum of three to four years before repotting into a slightly larger container.

TIP
The bigger the container, the lighter the material it should be made from – think wicker or plastic. This is particularly relevant if the plant is going to be moved around fairly often.

MOSS TOPPINGS

* The two most common types of moss to use are flat moss, which is green, or reindeer moss, which is white and a type of lichen.
* Mist the moss every time you water the plant. If it dries out, give it a good soaking and its colour will come back.
* Don't collect moss youself – buy it from garden centres or florists.
* Moss may attract unsightly sciarid flies (see pages 168) if your plant is somewhere dark and damp.
* Instead of using moss as a surface dressing, try slate chippings, pebbles, gravel or wood chips. They will help your plant to retain moisture, although not as well as moss.

CONTAINER MATERIALS

Below left:
The planting scheme in this fishbowl terrarium features *Crassula ovata* (money tree), *Aloe vera* (Barbados aloe), an *Echeveria* and ferns on a bed of gravel.

Below right:
Humidity-loving plants in wooden pots: *Zamioculcas zamiifolia* (fern arum), *Ficus microcarpa* 'Ginseng' (Indian laurel) and *Asparagus densiflorus* 'Myersii' (plume asparagus).

The beauty of container planting is that by trying out different shapes, materials, finishes and colours, you can quickly alter the finished look of your arrangement. Do this over time and your planting design can evolve along with your changing tastes and general trends.

Your containers can make a massive difference to the overall mood of your display – a classic terracotta long tom, for example, has a very different feel from a high-shine metal planter.

It's now easy to source containers in as many materials and finishes as you can name. Whether your preference is for earthy hewn woods, woven baskets and aged terracotta or slick brass, copper and marble-effect finishes, someone out there will have the container of your dreams.

When choosing containers, look at both the shape and shades of your plant. Do you want the pot to disappear into the background, so the plant takes centre stage, or do you want to use it to reflect the plant's shape or offset its colours?

Take a look at the area where you intend to place the pots. The two most effective approaches are to have pots that either complement the space and so blend in, or wildly contrast with it, thereby making a statement. For a group of plants, you'll need to decide if you want pots of the same material and size, or different sizes for each container, or perhaps different styles but unite them by ensuring they're all in the same finish. Each decision will make a difference to the final look.

TIP

Create a simple focal-point display by planting up an attractive bowl with seasonally appropriate bulbs: think *Narcissus* 'Tête-à-Tête', which is a dwarf daffodil, in spring; *Cyclamen persicum* (Persian cyclamen) at Christmas.

This page:
These crackle-glazed and chalky terracotta pots are planted with *Peperomia rotundifolia*, *Echeveria agavoides* 'Taurus' and *Pteris cretica* var. *albolineata* (white-striped Cretan brake).

This page:
A small terrarium lends itself to an intimate planting scheme. From left: *Peperomia* (radiator plant), *Crassula ovata* (money tree) and *Echeveria*, finished with *Cladonia rangiferina* (reindeer moss).

Originally a feature of over-furnished Victorian parlours, the terrarium is undergoing a serious revival. This is in no small part down to the fact that the glass vessel conveniently creates a microclimate, meaning it can be positioned pretty much anywhere, as long as the plants inside get sufficient light and warmth.

Terrariums are good-looking objects, and clever planting that plays on the relationship between the lines and shape of the terrarium and the plants inside makes a strong design statement. The impact will be greater if you use either a single plant, such as *Echeveria elegans* (Mexican gem), or create a mini landscape with two or three varieties of plants, such as *Asparagus setaceus* (asparagus fern) with a *Nertera granadensis* (bead plant) or some small cacti. Species of *Tillandsia* (air plant) are a great choice for a minimalist-style terrarium because they take their water and nutrition from the air.

RETURN OF THE TERRARIUM

Above left:
A fishbowl works surprisingly well as a simple terrarium. Add interest with different shapes of succulents and cacti.

Below:
An open terrarium allows for attractive plant overspill, such as trailing plants draped over the edge or plants growing out of the top, like this cactus.

TOP TERRARIUM PLANTS

* *Aloe*
* *Begonia rex* (fan plant)
* *Chlorophytum comosum* (spider plant)
* *Crassula ovata* (money tree)
* Ferns (smaller forms)
* *Hedera* (ivy)
* *Hypoestes phyllostachya* (polka dot plant)
* *Peperomia caperata* (emerald ripple)
* *Sansevieria trifasciata* (mother-in-law's tongue)
* *Tillandsia* (air plant)

Note: Air plants, ivies and ferns will all do especially well in closed terrariums.

This page:
A grouping of geometric terrariums, planted with *Asparagus setaceus* (asparagus fern), a selection of succulents, *Sansevieria trifasciata* 'Golden Hahnii' (mother-in-law's tongue) and *Asplenium nidus* (bird's nest fern).

PLANTING TERRARIUMS

✳ For closed terrariums, choose plants that prefer low to medium light levels and moist potting compost.

✳ Open terrariums are like low-maintenance mini gardens, where the plants need higher light levels and more frequent watering.

✳ Drainage is key in open terrariums. Put in a 1–3cm (½–1in) layer of gravel, depending on the size of the terrarium, to the bottom before adding the potting compost.

✳ Choose plants with small leaves, slow rates of growth and a high tolerance of humidity.

✳ Experiment with your design ideas outside the terrarium first – it's much easier to make changes when you have a bit of space.

✳ You can buy miniature long-handled tools for planting and maintaining a terrarium, but an improvised tool kit comprising a fork and spoon, long-handled tweezers and a chopstick or two can be just as effective.

✳ Finish your arrangement with an attractive layer of moss, gravel or small pieces of bark.

✳ Once everything is in place, use a clean, dry cloth to gently wipe the inside of the glass.

Groups of terrariums work really well, so experiment with using them in the same design but in different sizes, or have a collection with a similar theme, such as three or four vintage apothecary bottles. Mix and match your vessels, from fishbowls to Kilner (Mason) jars, hurricane lamps to glass cloches. Just remember to choose glass-sided containers that will comfortably enclose the plants to help create that essential microclimate, restrict any draughts and allow you to see what is growing inside. As to where to put terrariums, they work really well on desks and dining tables, or as decorative features in their own right on a display shelf or a high-standing lamp table.

Terrariums need virtually little or no maintenance, depending on whether they are opened or closed – closed terrariums create their own water cycle, meaning they basically look after themselves. Any maintenance issues are more about keeping the glass nice and clean to show off the plants at their best.

TIP
Zeoponic is a newly developed form of water-retaining gravel that Ian likes to use for both terrarium and normal container planting. Keep an eye open for it – it will be coming to a garden centre near you soon.

This page:
Using a small terrarium as a
container can turn a single
plant, such as this *Sansevieria
trifasciata* 'Golden Hahnii'
(mother-in-law's tongue),
into a statement piece.

DESIGNING
WITH PLANTS

WHERE TO START

When deciding on a planting scheme, it works well if you are able to treat your plants as part of the overall room design, rather than as an add-on. That said, however, many of us decorate our homes piecemeal, room by room, meaning that the elements that bring real personality to a space tend to come some time after the hours spent poring over paint charts and choosing furniture.

First, take a good look at the space where you want the plants to go, to get a sense of its overall feel and arrangement. What have been your design influences? What style of furniture do you have? What kind of art is on display? What is your main colour scheme? Accent colours? Where, exactly, are you hoping to put the plants?

Next, collect images of plants you are drawn to, as well as containers and stands that you like, plus planting ideas that appeal – Pinterest is a useful tool for this. Light is incredibly important for a plant's survival so, before you buy, research whether your proposed location will meet the lighting requirements of your selected plants. You also have to decide on the care, commitment and time you are willing to give. There is absolutely no point in coming up with a striking 'indoor jungle' scheme, say, if, realistically, you are not the kind of person who is going to regularly dust down, prune and correctly water the plants.

You really don't need to have masses of plants to make a statement – it all comes down to how they are arranged and displayed. And remember that the space between your plants is as important as the plants themselves. Choosing plants of the same colour or perhaps using the same container in different sizes will create a cohesive design.

Another point to consider is whether you have a view of a garden or other green landscape. A really successful design scheme can involve bringing that exterior inside by planting around the window to frame the view. (Conversely, if you are facing a brick wall, you can screen the view.) This has the effect of both extending and reflecting the outside world. Adding a few elements that you would normally expect to find outdoors, such as weathered terracotta pots or exterior planters, is another neat way of linking indoors and out.

In terms of current design trends, it's all about the group. The days of a solitary stand-alone plant have gone – unless, of course, we mean a beautiful indoor tree or a huge feature plant that can act as a living sculpture. Grouping is a really simple styling trick, but its impact can be huge. We prefer to group our plants or containers in odd numbers – three, five, seven and so on.

TIP

If you're in any doubt about a design approach, keep your ideas clean, simple and tidy.

Above:
Create an eye-catching still life by planting indoor plants in complementary containers and combining them with striking objects, such as these three *Aloe* *variegata* (partridge breast aloe), an *Asparagus setaceus* (asparagus fern), a *Spathiphyllum wallisii* (peace lily) and an *Asplenium nidus* (bird's nest fern),

Other key design styles that we think are also really worth a try are terrariums – after all, everyone loves a self-contained, self-sufficient indoor garden; hanging plants with the aid of macramé and sky planters; and landscaping shelves, mantelpieces or windowsills with a considered grouping of plants and other *objets*.

PLANT LANDSCAPING

If you are grouping plants together to create a landscape effect, it's good to work with contrasts. Go for opposites: tall uprights, such as a *Ficus*, with low-growing bushy plants like *Epipremnum aureum* (devil's ivy); or a small-leaved plant, such as a *Peperomia caperata* (emerald ripple), next to one with broader leaves, perhaps a *Spathiphyllum wallisii* (peace lily). Alternatively, choose plants with different shades of foliage and add in a few feature flowering plants that pick up on the leaf colours.

Wooden beads — reminiscent of
nature, travels and texture

A living wall at L'Atelier
De Joel Robuchon, Covent
Garden, London

Sunflowers in bloom

Eames Black Wire Chair, Vitra

Architectural splendour —
Monstera deliciosa

A mini in Havana, Cuba

Princess of Wales Conservatory,
Kew Gardens, London

St Pancras Building,
King's Cross, London

A white house beneath
a blue sky in Cyprus

Paul Smith — an inspirational
fashion and design hero

The Yves Saint Laurent Garden,
Marrakech, Morocco

Peraliya Budha Statue,
Tsunami Memorial, Sri Lanka

Orange Panton Chair, Vitra

The Living Workstation at
RHS Chelsea Flower Show 2011

Movie Colony Palms, Palm
Springs, California

The stained glass
at the Ivy Restaurant,
Covent Garden, London

A herb table

Kinder catwalk, London Fashion
Week 2011, Autumn/Winter

SCALE & CONTRAST

Scale really is a brilliant device to play around with, and if you use it well, you don't need an enormous amount of space in which to be creative with your planting. Emphasizing the contrast between little and large, such as pairing two different plants with similar foliage but of totally different sizes – for example, a *Howea forsteriana* (Kentia palm) with a *Washingtonia robusta* (Mexican fan palm) or a *Sansevieria trifasciata* with a *S. cylindrica* – is a simple but effective design trick.

For a group planting scheme that packs a punch, be creative with your containers or plant choices. Groupings offer endless possibilities for developing an arrangement. They can also form a focal point in a room that previously had none or set the decorative tone.

There are several different ways to achieve such a scheme. Just think about the infinite varieties of container shapes, sizes, colours and materials available. Add to that the range of plants you might pick and you can see how much fun you can have creating a mix-and-match scheme.

Containers can create very different design themes, from vintage chic to slick minimalism. To give a scheme coherence, aim for a little consistency in some part of it, whether in the materials of the containers, their shape or the plants themselves – a single variety or plants from the same family, for example. Alternatively, choose a colour theme for your pots – think pastels or primaries, neons or monochromes.

Look outside for plant inspiration. Public gardens and parks are all about mixed planting schemes, with various plants of different shapes, colours and sizes bringing out the best in each other. Such an approach can be translated into a striking houseplant arrangement.

Below:
Put plants together with similar foliage shades, like this *Aeonium arboreum* 'Atropurpureum' (houseleek tree) and *Begonia rex*, for a coherent look.

Right:
Pair a tall plant, such as *Ficus cyathistipula*, with a squat one, like *Aglaonema* 'Silver Queen' (Chinese evergreen). Similar leaf shapes and containers give unity.

TOP TEN STAND-ALONE PLANTS

* *Beaucarnea recurvata* (elephant's foot)
* *Dracaena fragrans* (corn plant)
* *Fatsia japonica* (Japanese aralia)
* *Ficus benjamina* (weeping fig)
* *Ficus lyrata* (fiddle-leaf fig)
* *Howea forsteriana* (Kentia palm)
* *Monstera deliciosa* (Swiss cheese plant)
* *Philodendron scandens* (heart-leaf philodendron)
* *Schefflera* (umbrella tree)
* *Yucca elephantipes* (spineless yucca)

SYMMETRY & REPETITION

Below left:
Placing a pair of matching plants, such as these *Anigozanthos* (kangaroo paw), at either end of a mantelpiece, shelf or table, is a simple design trick that will please the eye.

Below right:
A mixed planting scheme of *Echeveria elegans* (Mexican gem), *Crassula ovata* 'Gollum' (money tree), *C. ovata* and *Peperomia rotundifolia* is given consistency with similarly finished containers.

If you really don't feel confident enough about experimenting with different looks, then there are two very simple tricks of the trade you can use that will always result in a successful display: symmetry and repetition. They are straightforward but effective devices and pretty much foolproof. Think about a pair of matching *Spathiphyllum wallisii* (peace lily) at either end of a mantelpiece, or the same single plant, such as *Zamioculcas zamiifolia* (fern arum), in identical planters lined up on the treads of a staircase.

The reason that symmetry and repetition work so well is that they please the eye: a symmetrical display looks 'tidy', while one plant used over and again creates impact. A lone *Phalaenopsis* (moth orchid) can appear insignificant, whereas a pair looks deliberate and four makes a statement.

Similarly, small plants such as *Aloe vera* (Barbados aloe) can sometimes disappear into the background of a room, but massed together, they will command attention.

Using repetition, whether of the plant variety or the planting method, creates a feeling of abundance and generosity in a decorative scheme. A large planter filled with several of the same variety of *Carex morrowii* 'Variegata' (sedge) or *Nephrolepis exaltata* 'Bostoniensis' (Boston fern), for example, makes for a fabulous centrepiece. Plants placed symmetrically on shelves or across the tops of cupboards can have the effect of giving a sharp, finished look to a room. In fact, if you are a novice plantsperson, you could decide to make symmetry or repetition – or even both – the foundation of your first display.

This page:
A line-up of planters
in alternating styles is a
simple design device for
displaying a collection
of plants from the same
family, in this case, ferns.

This page:
Put a spare surface to good use by displaying a mixed planting scheme interspersed with artwork. From left: *Epipremnum aureum* (devil's ivy), *Asplenium nidus* (bird's nest fern), an *Echeveria*, *Nephrolepis exaltata* 'Bostoniensis' (Boston fern), *Philodendron scandens* (heart-leaf philodendron), *Asparagus densiflorus* 'Myersii' (plume asparagus), *Peperomia rotundifolia*, *Ficus elastica* (rubber plant) and *Philodendron scandens* (heart-leaf philodendron) again.

This page:
Wall-hung box shelves are a neat way of framing small plants like *Kalanchoe sexangularis*, *Senecio rowleyanus* (string of beads), *Sempervivum tectorum* (common houseleek) and *Crassula perforata* (string of buttons), as well as keeping them out of harm's way.

Above left:
Bushy *Chlorophytum comosum* (spider plant) and ferns are given a sharper finish by being displayed in a minimalist plant stand.

Above right:
Vintage hampers used to display *Philodendron scandens* (heart-leaf philodendron), ferns and *Rhipsalis paradoxa* (chain cactus).

ALTERNATIVE DISPLAYS

There are as many different ways to display your houseplants as there are plants you can use. On the following pages, we look at some of our favourites, but there's no doubt that if you put your mind to it, you will come up with some original ideas of your own. Just keep in mind the size, shape and colour of your container and where you want to position it in the room, then decide how inventively you can make the different elements work together.

Single-plant shelves

Tiny, individual shelves, with just enough room for one pot, or decorative wall sconces are a really attractive way to present plants, especially in an awkward space. You can arrange a series of floating shelves on a wall, adding to them over time as you build up your plant collection. For the affordable DIY version, get a timber yard to cut the wood to size for you. Alternatively, seek out companies that specialize in home accessories (see pages 169–70).

Box shelves

Box shelves are a variation of the floating shelf. They effectively frame the item that's placed inside – in this case a plant in a pot – transforming it into a statement display. Box shelves work particularly

Above:
Make the most of a dramatic trailer, such as this *Rhipsalis paradoxa* (chain cactus), by investing in a stand that suits the growth style of a particular plant.

Right:
A collection of ferns teamed with a *Rhipsalis baccifera* (mistletoe cactus) is shown off to perfection in a glass display cabinet.

Hanging planters

At the mention of hanging plants, most people instantly hark back to the macramé planters that were so in favour during the hippy heyday of the 1970s. Now they are back in vogue among the hipster contingent.

Modern macramé planters can look fantastic when styled well. Try grouping them together or hang them in a line, at slightly different heights. Or play off their handmade feel against a slick, contemporary interior. Take a look at the work of British jewellery designer Eleanor Bolton (see page 169), who has created a collection of knotted rope planters in a range of both monochrome and contemporary accent colours that effectively style your plants for you.

Hanging planters aren't just made out of macramé, however; you can now find them in a variety of styles and materials, from cute glass baubles for air plants to modernist ceramic pieces. Then there are the larger-scale, flat 'hanging trays' that allow you to display a group of plants together – IKEA does a good affordable version.

Although hanging planters are a wonderful way of displaying plants at a different viewpoint, they're not just suited to homes that have high ceilings – a low hanging plant positioned in the corner of a room is particularly eye-catching because it is so unexpected.

Wall planters

Effectively pots attached directly to the wall, these planters are the perfect solution if you don't have many available flat surfaces for displaying your plants. They work well in spaces where there is a lot of passing traffic, such as the kitchen, hallway or bathroom, because they are securely held in place out of the way. As with floating or box shelves, they suit awkward or dead spaces, too – try positioning them in a vertical line up a tall wall, in the gap next to a door or a window frame, above a bedside table and so on.

well in children's rooms because the box helps to protect the plants from any accidental knocks. Used singly, these shelves create impact, but you can also add to them over time without reducing their appeal.

Box shelves are easy to come by in good interiors stores or on the internet. Don't forget to double-check dimensions to make sure they are large enough to accommodate your chosen plant and its container.

Peg boards

Remember those holey boards of plywood that your Dad used for hanging his tools from hooks in the garden shed or garage? Well, it's time to reclaim them for your plants. Spray-painted or varnished, then accessorized with a selection of wall planters attached with 'S' hooks, they make an adaptable display area that is both portable and interchangeable.

Living walls

These are essentially vertical gardens. A few years back, when living walls first came into vogue, their proponents used them for elaborate planting schemes to cover the outside of buildings or disguise ugly walls in a garden. Now the whole idea has been shrunk down to a domestic scale and you can buy ingenious wall-hanging planters that enable you to create your own indoor living wall.

You could, of course, be very ambitious and plant an entire wall from floor to ceiling, but a more manageable approach is to view your living wall as you would a large mirror or painting, and invest in a planter of an appropriate size and scale. Make sure you attach it securely to the wall, then simply plant it up. Trailing plants such as *Epipremnum aureum* (devil's ivy), *Tradescantia* (wandering Jew) and *Rhipsalis baccifera* (mistletoe cactus) suit this approach especially well.

Plant stands

Forget their 'granny' associations – plant stands are a neat and efficient way of giving a floor-standing plant an extra design dimension. They are also a useful device for introducing height to a floor-based scheme. Whether it's the retro, wire-frame look that interests you or the slicker feel of an integrated planter and stand, there is a design out there for you. Alternatively, you can, of course, play around with placing a large pot on a small side table or low stool to create a similar effect.

RIGHT PLANT, RIGHT ROOM

LIVING SPACES

For most of us, the living room is the showcase of our homes, where we express our personal style. It is often the room that people choose first when deciding where to make their decorative mark on a property. As well as being a personal place of relaxation, it is also the main 'public-facing' room in our homes, the space where we welcome in other people.

Houseplants can have an enormous impact here because living rooms, by the nature of their layout and usual design, offer plenty of areas and opportunities for creative planting arrangements. Just think of the surfaces and parts of the living room that can make welcome homes to a houseplant: mantelpieces, windowsills, shelves, corners, side tables – the permutations are as endless as your imagination.

If you spend a lot of time in your living room, and you've always hankered after a plant that's a real show stopper, this is probably the place to put it. A mature *Ficus benjamina* (weeping fig), *Philodendron bipinnatifidum* (horsehead philodendron), *Dracaena marginata* (Madagascar dragon tree), *Beaucarnea recurvata* (elephant's foot) or *Euphorbia tirucalli* (finger tree) are all real conversation pieces.

Alternatively, if your living room is spacious enough, you could go to town with creative groupings by clustering together different-sized, floor-based architectural palms, to create a focal point, or by dotting an arrangement of individually potted succulents along the mantelpiece instead of the typical collection of unremarkable knick-knacks.

Even better, choose plants in foliage colours that complement and enhance your favourite ornaments to create a living still life. The stems of trailing plants such as *Hedera helix* 'Sagittifolia' (English ivy) or *Rhipsalis paradoxa* (chain cactus) look dramatic draped over the edge of shelves and high cupboards, while a terrarium is a bold, self-contained piece of feature planting that's perfect for a coffee or side table.

A good piece of house planting really can complete the look of your living room, provided you consider the aesthetic impact of a planting scheme on the overall space and are also conscious of the practical growing requirements of the plants that you are picking in terms of light and heat.

FIVE OF THE BEST TRAILING PLANTS
* *Epipremnum aureum* (devil's ivy)
* *Hedera helix* (English ivy)
* *Mikania scandens* (climbing hemp vine)
* *Rhipsalis baccifera* (mistletoe cactus)
* *Tradescantia* (wandering Jew)

LARGE-SCALE DISPLAYS

Above:
This bold display evokes a Victorian hothouse. From left: *Dracaena marginata* (Madagascar dragon tree); terrarium of succulents; *Ficus microcarpa* 'Ginseng' (Indian laurel); *Ficus benjamina* (weeping fig); *Euphorbia tirucalli* (finger tree); *Asparagus densiflorus* 'Myersii' (plume asparagus); *Ficus elastica* 'Decora' (rubber plant); *Howea forsteriana* (Kentia palm); *Philodendron xanadu*; and *Peperomia rotundifolia*.

Right:
Groupings of odd numbers are pleasing to the eye and are a simple but effective design tool to use with plants. From left: *Howea forsteriana* (Kentia palm); *Washingtonia* x *filibusta* (Washington palm); *Howea forsteriana* (Kentia palm); and *Trachycarpus fortunei* (Chinese windmill palm).

The living room is usually the biggest room in the home, which is why it lends itself to large-scale displays. A large-scale display is one that is either tall or bold, or involves a grouping of several different plants and containers.

This type of planting design can serve several purposes: to create a focal point in a room that previously didn't have one; to separate and screen off different areas within the room; to disguise unsightly views; or simply to act as a beautiful piece of living sculpture.

FIVE STATEMENT FLOWERING PLANTS
These bold beauties will bring a sense of drama to any setting.

* *Anthurium scherzerianum* (flamingo flower)
* *Medinilla magnifica* (rose grape)
* *Spathiphyllum wallisii* (peace lily)
* *Tillandsia cyanea* (pink quill)
* *Vanda* orchids

Above:
A mix of *Rhipsalis baccifera* (mistletoe cactus), *Epipremnum aureum* (devil's ivy), *Philodendron scandens* (heart-leaf philodendron) and *Asplenium nidus* (bird's nest fern) makes an eye-catching shelfie above the single pots scattered below.

Above right:
Plants from the same family create a coherent display. This line-up includes *Chamaedorea elegans* (parlour palm), *Rhapis excelsa* (bamboo palm) and *Washingtonia* x *filibusta* (Washington palm), with a floor-standing *Howea forsteriana* (Kentia palm).

Be aware that tall, architectural, floor-standing plants, such as a *Monstera deliciosa* (Swiss cheese plant) or a *Carnegiea gigantea* (saguaro), can be quite expensive to buy because it will have taken the grower several years to get them to maturity. Having said that, these are also the plants that really make a statement in themselves, so you do in fact get a lot of bang for your buck in terms of making an impact.

However, if cost is a real consideration, another way to create height (if that's the way you want to go in a large-scale display) is to use your pieces of furniture to give medium- or smaller-sized plants a bit of a 'leg up'. Try grouping them together on a side table or stool, or use a plant stand to achieve the same effect. Alternatively, invest in some tall, open shelves, which you can put to use as a room divider, and fill with row upon row of individually potted plants – a straightforward idea that looks really striking.

Or how about turning the height idea on its head and look to the ceiling, instead of the floor, as your starting point? There are a plethora of different styles of hanging planters now available, in materials as varied as macramé, metal and marble, which you can attach to hooks in the ceiling, thereby creating an arrangement at eye-level. This is also a great technique for using plants as a screening device, either by repeating the same type of plant all in a line or by hanging the plants at different heights. Orchid 'curtains' work really well for this, too. They look spectacular and are surprisingly simple to achieve with *Vanda* orchids, which behave a bit like air plants, and can be simply hung from hooks at varying heights.

This page:
An occasional table is perfect for an unrestrained group planting. From left: *Platycerium bifurcatum* (staghorn fern), *Ficus elastica* (rubber plant), *Euphorbia tirucalli* (finger tree), *Asparagus densiflorus* 'Myersii' (plume asparagus), *Philodendron scandens* (heart-leaf philodendron), *Aglaonema modestum* (Chinese evergreen) and *Epipremnum aureum* (devil's ivy).

Left:
For such a small plant, a *Tillandsia* (air plant) makes a big statement and, because it lives on air, it can be dotted in and around other objects. The examples here slot in neatly with an intimate display of animal bones.

Right:
Draw attention to diminutive plants such as this *Echeveria* and smaller varieties like this *Asplenium nidus* (bird's nest fern) by using decorative containers or eye-catching framing devices.

INTIMATE DISPLAYS

LIVING SPACES

69

Intimate displays are all about creating close-up interest. They are not concerned with the wham-bam effect of a striking, large-scale arrangement, but more about attention to detail.

Think about the colour, texture and design of your containers – at this level they are often as significant as the plants – as well as the outline form, foliage tones and leaf shape of the plants you want to use. Think of the difference in look between an *Opuntia microdasys* (bunny ears cactus), an *Aloe variegata* (partridge breast aloe) and a *Nephrolepis exaltata* (sword fern) to see what we mean.

Intimate displays can bring life to forgotten corners: the edge of a mantelpiece, a narrow spot on a windowsill, the top of a piano. They are also a useful device for drawing the eye to interesting, unusual or quirky details within a room.

Even though the dimensions you are working with are considerably smaller than those of a large-scale display, you can still put to use some of the same design techniques: grouping plants of different heights and ways of growing, such as a small upright *Ficus elastica* (rubber plant), a bushy *Asparagus setaceus* (asparagus fern) and a draping *Philodendron scandens* (heart-leaf philodendron), for example, or selecting those with complementary foliage shades, like a *Begonia rex* (fan plant) and an *Aeonium tabulaeforme* (flat-topped aeonium).

Consider as well the style, material and colour of the furniture on which the arrangement is displayed. A group of tall cacti will give a vintage rosewood cabinet, for example, a moody look; a couple of bold *Hippeastrum* (amaryllis) will provide added impact; while a bowl of scented *Hyacinthus* (hyacinth) will lighten it up entirely.

A little container garden can make a very effective intimate display, but remember that it will be easier to look after if you use the same type of plant or choose varieties with similar light and watering needs. Then there is the current design favourite, the terrarium, which now comes in a large range of shapes and materials.

MANTELS & FIREPLACES

Below left:
Even a narrow mantel can be used as a display surface, provided you choose small varieties of plants, such as *Tillandsia* (air plant).

Below right:
The texture of this basket complements the plants growing inside: *Howea forsteriana* (Kentia palm), *Washingtonia* x *filibusta* (Washington palm) and *Rhapis excelsa* (bamboo palm).

Even if a fireplace isn't used for its original purpose, in most living rooms it will still be the main focal point. It is also really easy to style up with plants. If it is still in use, choose heat-tolerant plants such as succulents, cacti and *Tillandsia* (air plant), and avoid trailing plants.

Individual plants in separate pots allow you to rearrange the display at will, while a trough of complementary plants creates a simple, stylish statement. Symmetrical mantel displays can work well, as can repetitive designs, or divide the space into a series of small vignettes, introducing plants alongside ornaments. A mantel can also take one bold plant, such as *Anthurium scherzerianum* (flamingo flower), *Zantedeschia aethiopica* (calla lily), a *Dendrobium* orchid or *Medinilla magnifica* (rose grape).

For the hearth, gather together pots of tall and squat plants, such as *Zamioculcas zamiifolia* (fern arum), *Calathea makoyana* (peacock plant) and *Epipremnum aureum* (devil's ivy). For the grate, try *Zamioculcas zamiifolia* as the backbone, *Rhipsalis baccifera* (mistletoe cactus) for trailing, plus *Aglaonema* 'Silver Queen' (Chinese evergreen) for foliage colour.

RECIPE: EASY-CARE MANTEL DISPLAY

2 *Begonia rex* (fan plant)
1 *Beaucarnea recurvata* (elephant's foot)
1 *Peperomia caperata* (emerald ripple)
2 *Echeveria setosa* (Mexican firecracker)

This page:
Houseplants are
interspersed with favourite
ornaments for a more
personal display, with,
from left: *Aloe vera* an
Echeveria, Peperomia rotundifolia
and *Zamioculcas zamiifolia*
(fern arum) on the mantel,
and *Platycerium bifurcatum*
(staghorn fern) decorating
the hearth.

This page:
Placing single plants in separate pots makes it easy to rearrange a display. From left: *Aeonium arboreum* 'Atropurpureum', *Begonia rex*, *Beaucarnea recurvata* (elephant's foot), *Begonia rex*, *Peperomia rotundifolia*, *Echeveria agavoides* 'Taurus' and *Pteris cretica* var. *albolineata* (white-striped Cretan brake).

OTHER DISPLAY IDEAS

Put side and lamp tables to good use by enlisting them as a supporting surface for an eclectic cluster of mix-and-match plants, positioning taller plants at the centre or back of the display, with smaller ones around the edges or front.

Draw the eye upwards by using the tops of cupboards and high shelves as plant zones. This approach works particularly well in rooms with high ceilings, or if the furniture in question has interesting detailing. Plants on a high shelf can draw attention to architectural details nearby, such as cornicing and coving, picture rails, panels or plasterwork.

Plants can populate shelves in a variety of ways, acting as spacers between collections of books or as a means of highlighting some of your favourite decorative items. For example, make a line of matching plants the sole occupant and, therefore, the key feature of one shelf, or employ trailing and draping plants – think *Aporocactus flagelliformis* (rat's tail cactus), *Hedera helix* 'Eva' (English ivy) or *Ficus sagitatta* 'Variegata' – as a means of softening up the rigid, hard lines of a shelving system. The possibilities are endless.

Don't feel, though, that you have to confine your planting to the obvious living room locations and put your mind to how you can use unexpected or alternative display areas for your plants. Engage other pieces of furniture to be a part of your scheme. A couple of plants on a drinks trolley, for example, can really bring it to life – and it works even better if the plants are herbs with the added benefit of being able to perk up your cocktails. You can also use spare chairs, tray tables, small step ladders and piles of magazines as surfaces on which to place a pot.

How and where you display your plants is all about being a bit relaxed in your approach. After all, if you don't like an idea or think it doesn't work, you can always shift them to another spot.

Top left:
Hanging planters are handy when free surfaces are few and far between. From left: *Euphorbia tirucalli* (finger tree) and *Peperomia rotundifolia*.

Bottom left:
A drinks trolley is a unique display for *Washingtonia* x *filibusta* (Washington palm) and *Asparagus densiflorus* 'Myersii' (plume asparagus).

Top right:
Use spare chairs and side tables to display plants, such as these succulents, including *Aloe vera* (Barbados aloe) and *Echeveria agavoides* 'Taurus'.

Bottom right:
A step stool has been put to good use as a plant stand, planted here with, from top, *Ficus carica* (common fig) and *Peperomia rotundifolia*.

RECIPES: THE PERFECT SHELFIE

2 *Sansevieria trifasciata* (mother-in-law's tongue)
2 *Zamioculcas zamiifolia* (fern arum)
3 *Epipremnum aureum* (devil's ivy)
3 *Beaucarnea recurvata* (elephant's foot)

OR

3 *Rhipsalis paradoxa* (chain cactus)
3 *Sansevieria trifasciata* (mother-in-law's tongue)
2 *Beaucarnea recurvata* (elephant's foot)
2 *Maranta leuconeura* (prayer plant)

SEASONAL FLOWERS

Bulbs and flowering pot plants bring additional colour and variety to indoor planting schemes. Most spring bulbs suit being planted up en masse in a large container, but they also grow well and look rather good in a hanging planter. The larger flowering bulbs such as *Hippeastrum* (amaryllis) or *Zantedeschia aethiopica* (calla lily) are usually so bold and dramatic that you don't need to do much to make them look good – just place them in a position that shows off their sculptural lines.

Above:
Bring outdoor plants, such as *Hydrangea macrophylla* (common hydrangea), indoors for a short period for some seasonal colour.

TIP
....
As a general rule, flowering plants need more light than foliage varieties. Bear this in mind when deciding where to display them. Position in a bright spot and turn the pots regularly.

YEAR-ROUND FLOWERING PLANTS

SPRING

Clivia miniata (Natal lily), *Crocus chrysanthus* (Golden crocus), *Hyacinthus* (hyacinth), *Narcissus cyclamineus* 'Tête-à-Tête' (narcissus), *Primula vulgaris* (primrose).

SUMMER

Argyranthemum frutescens (marguerite), *Centaurea cyanus* (cornflower), *Lavandula* (lavender), *Paeonia* (peony), *Rosa* (rose), *Rosmarinus officinalis* (rosemary).

AUTUMN

Calluna vulgaris (heather), *Chrysanthemum morifolium* (pot chrysanthemum), *Physalis alkekengi* (Chinese lantern), *Solanum capsicastrum* (winter cherry).

WINTER

Cyclamen persicum (Persian cyclamen), *Euphorbia pulcherrima* (poinsettia), *Hedera helix* (English ivy), *Hippeastrum* (amaryllis), *Ilex* (holly), *Jasminum nudiflorum* (winter jasmine), *Schlumbergera truncata* (Christmas cactus).

IDEAS FOR CHRISTMAS

* Line up miniature *Araucaria heterophylla* (Norfolk Island pine) and *Cyclamen persicum* (Persian cyclamen) dressed with moss. Or swap the trees for diminutive *Hedera helix* (English ivy), *Ilex* (holly) and *Rosa* (rose).

* Display bowls of *Hippeastrum* (amaryllis) underplanted with *Ilex* (holly) and *Hedera helix* (English ivy) on tables and ledges.

* Individual pots of *Hippeastrum* work brilliantly placed up a staircase.

* *Euphorbia pulcherrima* (poinsettia) looks wonderful when displayed en masse.

* Group three Christmas trees (such as Norway spruce) of varied heights and decorate each one differently. Try wiring miniature terracotta pots of tiny *Cyclamen persicum* (Persian cyclamen) or *Rosa* (rose) onto the branches.

This page:
A group of miniature *Rosa* (rose) in complementary pots makes a pretty table-top display in summer. Put the plants back in the garden when they have finished flowering.

12
PLANTS
FOR LIVING
SPACES

Aechmea fasciata
Common name:
Urn plant
Light: Bright light
Care: Lightly water roots;
replenish water in its
reservoir when it dries out
Tips: Epsom salts and
bright light can be used
to induce a pinkish
orange bloom in spring

Araucaria heterophylla
Common name:
Norfolk Island palm
Light: High light levels
Care: Keep compost moist
Tips: Turn the plant
regularly to promote even
growth; trim only lower
branches, not from the top

Ficus lyrata
Common name:
Fiddle-leaf fig
Light: Bright to
moderate, indirect light
Care: Keep compost moist
Tips: Keep leaves clean
and polished, and
prune the top leaves
to promote bushiness

Ficus microcarpa 'Ginseng'
Common name:
Indian laurel
Light: Bright,
indirect light
Care: Keep moist;
mist regularly
Tips: Prune regularly to
retain the plant's shape;
prune back to 2 leaves
after 6–8 have grown

Begonia rex
Common name:
Fan plant
Light: Bright,
indirect light
Care: Water lightly;
keep moist
Tips: Nip off buds and
blossoms to help maintain
large, healthy leaves

Clivia miniata
Common name:
Natal lily
Light: Moderate light
Care: Keep compost
slightly moist
Tips: Keep in cool
temperatures to encourage
flowering in early spring

Schefflera elegantissima
Common name:
False aralia
Light: Moderate to bright,
indirect light
Care: Drench plant and
then allow surface compost
to dry before re-watering
Tips: Repot annually in
spring, but don't put in
too large a pot

Echeveria elegans
Common name:
Mexican gem
Light: Bright light
Care: Keep slightly moist
Tips: Remove the offshoots
and propagate them to
prevent the pot from
becoming overcrowded

Medinilla magnifica
Common name:
Rose grape
Light: Bright,
filtered light
Care: High humidity;
water moderately
Tips: Prune the plant
back to half its size after
flowering to promote
future blossoms

Phalaenopsis
Common name:
Moth orchid
Light: Place in good light,
but not direct sunlight
Care: Tolerates high
humidity
Tips: Cut stem back to
second notch from the
base after flowering to
encourage future flowers

Streptocarpus hybrids
Common name:
Cape primrose
Light: Moderate to
bright light
Care: Keep compost moist
Tips: Keep in small
containers to prevent root
rot; pinch off old flowers
to encourage new growth

Tillandsia cyanea
Common name:
Pink quill
Light: Bright light
Care: Spray twice
weekly; keep moist
Tips: Keep cool in
winter to encourage
spring blooms

KITCHENS & EATING SPACES

It's said that the kitchen is the heart of the home, so why not show yours a little love with some creative planting? However, before you start on any scheme, it's always helpful to think about which plants might work the best in a particular space.

Although it might be something of a cliché, herbs are the obvious choice for a kitchen. They work on a practical level because they are an invaluable cooking ingredient, while their fragrance can also mask any unpleasant odours. Aesthetically, they can also create a really attractive feature – try placing a large container of mixed herbs on the table as part of a decorative setting, or plant individual varieties of herbs in separate matching containers and line them up along a shelf, a windowsill or, space permitting, a work surface.

The only thing that you should be aware of is that herbs do need a little care and attention. They like good light, and the different varieties can have quite particular watering requirements. Other edible plants such as the different *Citrus* species or *Capsicum annuum* (chilli pepper) are also attractive additions to a kitchen planting scheme.

There is something about that vibrant chlorophyll green of healthy, thriving, growing plants that just belongs in a kitchen – perhaps because it is usually the room that links to any

Above:
Indulge your sense of fun with the containers you choose. This llama-shaped pot makes a playful and original planter for a *Peperomia rotundifolia*.

Right:
Ferns, including this *Nephrolepis exaltata* 'Bostoniensis' (Boston fern), will thrive in the humid conditions found in a kitchen.

outside space there is. To make the most of that inside-outside flow, look out for plants that are able to tolerate the heat and humidity found in a kitchen – think *Asplenium* ferns and the various *Echeveria* succulents. *Chlorophytum comosum* (spider plant) and, perhaps surprisingly, *Phalaenopsis* (moth orchid) also enjoy the environs of a kitchen. As long as you find a bright spot for them, they will thrive.

Left:
Create your own indoor kitchen garden with a selection of edible plants, such as *Citrus japonica* (kumquat); *Citrus* x *microcarpa* (calamondin orange); mixed herbs and *Capsicum annuum* (chilli pepper).

Below:
A selection of plants at different heights – from left, *Aglaonema modestum* (Chinese evergreen), *Ficus lyrata* (fiddle-leaf fig), *Begonia rex* and *Philodendron xanadu* – adds interest to a formal dining space.

FIVE REALLY USEFUL INDOOR HERBS

The following herbs all prefer a light, bright position, such as a sunny windowsill. Ideally, check them every couple of days to see if they need watering because they really hate drying out. Misting them occasionally doesn't hurt, but make sure you don't over-water. Avoid buying supermarket herbs if at all possible – they are grown and treated in such a way as to last for only a short time. Instead, buy your plants from a garden centre.

* *Allium schoenoprasum* (chives)
* *Coriandrum sativum* (coriander/cilantro)
* *Mentha* (mint)
* *Ocimum basilicum* (basil)
* *Petroselinum crispum* (parsley)

Having something attractive to look at every day while going about our daily chores in the kitchen can lift the spirits no end. And it doesn't have to be an elaborate affair to produce the desired effect. Our absolutely favourite idea is to have one fairly substantial planter filled with a grouping of the same plants. A trug filled with a mix of *Asplenium* ferns with different foliage colours and leaf shapes looks fabulous, while a rush basket of grass-like *Carex morrowii* 'Variegata' (sedge) will gently waft in any breeze. Just make sure the container you choose is of a size that you can easily lift and carry in case you need to clear the decks – in a kitchen space, portable is practical.

Positioning your chosen display off-centre, at one corner or to one end of the kitchen table looks really effective. The stems of a trailing *Rhipsalis paradoxa* (chain cactus) or two draped over a corner or an edge is unexpected but striking. Likewise, try a collection of plants you wouldn't necessarily associate with a kitchen, such as the delicate-looking *Phalaenopsis* (moth orchid), which comes in a whole kaleidoscope of colours.

If the table is wide enough, put the space in the middle to good use with a neat, ordered line-up of plants. Be conscious of the scale of the plants you choose, though. There is nothing more annoying than not being able to see people seated around the table because of an arrangement that is either too tall or too broad.

TABLE TOPS

Above and below: Grouping together the same plants or plants of the same family in one large container makes for an impressive table-top display. A rush basket complements the group of *Beaucarnea recurvata* (elephant's foot) planted inside (above), while a selection of ferns lightens the look of a recycled rubber trug (below).

FIVE SUCCESSFUL KITCHEN PLANTS

* *Asparagus setaceus* (asparagus fern)
* *Chlorophytum comosum* (spider plant)
* *Ficus microcarpa* 'Ginseng' (Indian laurel)
* *Phalaenopsis* (moth orchid)
* *Soleirolia soleirolii* (mind-your-own-business)

This page:
The delicate-looking *Phalaenopsis* (moth orchid) is not a plant you would usually associate with a kitchen, but it makes a striking table-top display here, teamed with *Pteris cretica* var. *albolineata* (white-striped Cretan brake) and *Nephrolepis exaltata* 'Bostoniensis' (Boston fern), all in white containers.

Left:
Create a natural flow
between house and garden
by placing plants by a door,
such as this *Dracaena fragrans*
(corn plant), which has
the advantage of growing
slowly and staying narrow.

Right:
Ficus lyrata (fiddle-leaf fig),
one of the most eye-
catching houseplants,
thrives in a position by a
glass door or window, on
the threshold between
inside and out.

BRINGING THE OUTSIDE IN

Most indoor plants are evergreen, so having them
in your home means that even in the depths of
winter you will get a 'hit' of nature to lift your
spirits. And when the great outdoors is thriving
and growing, houseplants make the link between
inside and out. So play up your room with a
view and turn your kitchen into a bit of a garden
room. Add planting to those areas that connect
the outdoors with indoors, namely windows and
doors, to create a natural flow between the two.

Tuck one light-loving, floor-standing,
architectural plant such as *Ficus lyrata* (fiddle-leaf
fig) or *Dracaena marginata* (Madagascar dragon tree)
into a corner by the kitchen door. If you have the
space, be adventurous and create a sort of free-
form, 'modern conservatory' feel with a jungle of
mixed planting. Think hanging containers and
floor-standing planters, and perhaps introduce
another surface – some low steps, a plant stand
or a barstool, for example – to support plants of a
medium scale. Allow your grouping to spill into
the room a little for a relaxed feel.

Windows lend themselves to simple repetitive
line-ups. If the sill is wide enough, you have
a ready-made planting zone. If it's not, think
laterally. Hanging planters are a useful tool. You
could also put up a narrow shelf across the window
and add some little pots and plants – succulents and
trailers such as *Echeveria elegans* (Mexican gem) and
Hedera helix (English ivy) – along it. Alternatively,
buy a little herb planter (a co-ordinating drip tray
and pots), a narrow trough or an indoor window
box and position it directly in front of the window.
Asparagus setaceus (asparagus fern), *Ficus benjamina*
(weeping fig) and *Chlorophytum comosum* (spider
plant), in particular, favour this kind of position.

FIVE THRIVING THRESHOLD PLANTS
* *Araucaria heterophylla* (Norfolk Island pine)
* *Ficus lyrata* (fiddle-leaf fig)
* *Hedera helix* (English ivy)
* *Philodendron xanadu*
* *Tetrastigma voinierianum* (chestnut vine)

WORK SURFACES

Practical planting is probably your best bet for a kitchen work surface, placing herbs or other edibles within easy reach of the chef's prepping area and decorative plants out of the way.

Filling a garden trug with a selection of different herbs keeps them contained as well as looking good, while a cluster of individual pots of herbs is practical and pretty – even better if you have planted them up in vintage terracotta pots. Recycled tin cans with striking graphics – think Italian tomatoes or Greek olive oil – also lend themselves to a kitchen planting scheme. Place the containers on a large decorative tray or chopping board to hold the arrangement together.

Try to keep your work surface display organized and compact so it doesn't take up too much room. A neat line-up of the same style of container sums up this look, but it doesn't mean you can't be a little imaginative with it. Look at the materials you have used elsewhere in the kitchen – the work surfaces, tiles, cupboards, appliances and so on – and work with them when choosing your containers.

If your work surface space is really limited, remember that just one plant can have impact in a room if it is placed in the right position. Look to the end of your run of worktops or the corner of an island unit and use that as the spot for one beautiful, bold, eye-catching plant.

TIP

....

Avoid positioning plants, but herbs in particular, close to the cooker because of fluctuations in temperature.

Above left:
Containers with clean lines suit modern kitchens. From left: *Chlorophytum comosum* (spider plant), *Mentha* (mint) and *Ocimum basilicum* (basil).

Above right:
A garden trug filled with a selection of herbs is the logical choice for a planting on a kitchen worktop.

COMPACT PLANTS FOR WORKTOPS
* *Aloe vera* (Barbados aloe)
* *Echeveria elegans* (Mexican gem)
* *Mentha* species (mint)
* *Parodia chrysacanthion*
* *Zamioculcas zamiifolia* (fern arum)

This page:
A line-up of compact little
cacti makes a delightful but
unexpected display by the
kitchen sink.

This page:
Use colour co-ordinated containers to bring coherence to a shelving display of varied plants and pots. Clockwise, from top left: *Tradescantia* (wandering Jew), *Aloe vera* (Barbados aloe), *Maranta leuconeura* var. *erythroneura* (herringbone plant), a selection of succulents in the terrarium and *Peperomia rotundifolia*.

SHELVES

Positioning display plants on kitchen shelves at different heights adds interest and can give the impression of a very generous arrangement – even with a limited number of plants. Intersperse a set of shelves with plants of different shapes and sizes. If you think of it as a vertical garden, that will help you to create the arrangement. For example, have trailing plants dangling from the top shelves, place taller plants lower down to draw the eye up and balance it all out with bushy plants in the middle.

If your ceilings are high, make the most of the dead space above and position a shelf about 30–50cm (12–20in) below the ceiling. Fill it with pots of trailing plants, such as *Philodendron scandens* (heart-leaf philodendron) or *Epipremnum aureum* (devil's ivy), so they effectively drape down the wall.

Most kitchen-friendly plants are green, but you can pick up any accent colours or features you have in the room through your planters.

Above:
Shelves of terracotta long tom pots are an appealing choice and make a link between the kitchen and vegetable garden.

Below:
Create a 'vertical garden' by positioning plants at different heights on a shelf system.

TOP PLANTS FOR SHELF DISPLAYS
BUSHY:
* *Asparagus setaceus* (asparagus fern)
* *Asplenium nidus* (bird's nest fern)
TRAILING:
* *Epipremnum aureum* (devil's ivy)
* *Philodendron scandens* (heart-leaf philodendron)
* *Rhipsalis paradoxa* (chain cactus)

Left:
This orchid collection, including *Cattleya*, *Dendrobium* and *Zygopetalum*, suits this sunny position under a kitchen skylight because they are plants that like light and humidity.

Below left:
Quirky pots add personality to a small-scale display of *Hypoestes phyllostachya* (polka dot plant) and *Hedera helix* (English ivy).

OTHER IDEAS

If you're stuck for obvious planting places in your kitchen, slowly and carefully scan the whole room, from floor to ceiling, to see if you can see any little niches or unexpected spots to house a plant or two. The tops of cupboards, for example, lend themselves to plant displays, while a freestanding fridge would look all the better with some greenery featured on top.

Take advantage of any skylights and position light-loving plants, such as *Ficus benjamina* (weeping fig) or *Crassula ovata* (money tree), underneath them – you may need to add a narrow wall shelf in order to do this. Alternatively, attach a piece of decorative trellis to a wall and use it to hang planters from.

Recycled vintage kitchen equipment, such as casseroles and colanders, teapots and tankards, make for eye-catching details. If you want to expand on this idea, choose containers that either complement, match or pick up on any feature colours in the crockery you use.

If the kitchen is the family hub of the home, introduce some humour with planters in quirky shapes or designs: think animals, vegetables, retro prints and so on.

This page:
Build a tablescape by
pulling together a group
of individually potted-up
Philodendron scandens (heart-
leaf philodendron) and
Epipremnum aureum (devil's ivy).

12
PLANTS FOR KITCHENS & EATING SPACES

Anthurium missouri ('Anthcandol')
Common name: Flamingo flower
Light: Place in good light; avoid direct sunlight
Care: Water thoroughly and do not allow compost to dry out between watering
Tips: Repot annually in spring; keep leaves clean and polished

Crassula ovata
Common name: Money tree
Light: Needs plenty of light
Care: Tolerates high humidity; keep compost well drained
Tips: Plenty of light and fertilizer improves the leaf colour

Phalaenopsis 'Rio Grande'
Common name: Moth orchid
Light: Place in good light, but not direct sunlight
Care: Tolerates high humidity
Tips: Cut stem back to second notch from the base after flowering to encourage future flowers

Saintpaulia ionantha
Common name: African violet
Light: Moderate to bright, indirect sunlight
Care: Allow compost around the roots to dry out between waterings
Tips: These plants bloom and bloom; pinch off old flowers to encourage future flowers

Dendrobium speciosum
Common name: New South Wales rock lily
Light: Place in good light, but not direct sunlight
Care: Tolerates high humidity
Tips: Plenty of fertilizer and regular watering promotes flowering

Echeveria secunda var. *glauca*
Common name: Glaucous echeveria
Light: Place in a bright spot
Care: Needs well-drained compost; tolerates medium humidity
Tips: Pinch off the blooms to preserve the appearance of the rosettes

Kalanchoe blossfeldiana
Common name: Flaming Katy
Light: Place in good light, but not direct sunlight
Care: Water only when compost is dry
Tips: Pinch off blooms after the flowers fade to preserve the look of the plant

Nephrolepis exaltata 'Bostoniensis'
Common name: Boston fern
Light: Needs good light, but not direct sunlight
Care: Keep compost moist
Tips: Mist daily; trim off any broken or brown fronds

Schlumbergera truncata
Common name: Christmas cactus
Light: Indirect light
Care: Tolerates high humidity; keep compost well drained
Tips: Avoid over-watering, under-watering or other stress to prevent flowers from dropping

Epipremnum aureum
Common name: Devil's ivy
Light: Moderate to bright light
Care: Enjoys high humidity; compost should be kept moist, but do not over-water
Tips: Prune twice a year to keep the plant looking bushy and full

Spathiphyllum wallisii
Common name: Peace lily
Light: Likes good light, but can tolerate shade
Care: Thrives in higher humidity; keep compost moist
Tips: Remove flowering stems when the blooms ripen to green; keep leaves clean and polished

Stephanotis floribunda
Common name: Madagascar jasmine
Light: Plenty of bright light
Care: Needs well-drained compost; tolerates high humidity
Tips: Keep cool in winter and ensure high humidity from spring to promote flowering

SLEEPING SPACES

Our bedrooms are our sanctuaries, the most private spaces in our homes to which we retreat in order to recharge our batteries. However, few adults today get the optimum eight hours' sleep to function at their best, and insomnia is on the rise – it seems that we have lost the habit of good sleeping practices.

Creating a space where you can relax properly is a crucial part of developing what the experts call 'good sleep hygiene', and plants can have an important part to play in this. Not only do they look good, but they also help us to feel calm and act as natural air conditioners, gently raising humidity levels and improving air quality.

Look for plants that can cope with the slightly cooler temperatures and potentially lower light levels, and try to seek out the varieties that are proven toxin filters, such as *Philodendron scandens* (heart-leaf philodendron) and *Spathiphyllum wallisii* (peace lily). By happy coincidence, most of these plants are extremely attractive, with gently draping growth habits or softly wafting leaves, which means that they slot neatly into a bedroom with a laid-back look.

You can take this approach to the next level by seeking out some of the few plants that are night-time oxygenators; in other words, those plants that improve air quality while you sleep.

TOP NIGHT-TIME OXYGENATORS

Unlike most plants, the following behave counterintuitively, releasing oxygen at night instead of during the day. This is believed to be beneficial in a bedroom because it helps to improve the quality of the air we breathe while we're sleeping. The bonus is that these houseplants are all very striking and will simply look good wherever they are placed.

* *Aloe vera* (Barbados aloe)
* Bromeliads such as *Aechmea fasciata* (urn plant), *Guzmania lingulata* (scarlet star plant), *Tillandsia cyanea* (pink quill)
* *Dendrobium* orchids
* *Gerbera jamesonii* (Barberton daisy)
* *Hatiora gaertneri* (Easter cactus)
* *Phalaenopsis* (moth orchid)
* *Sansevieria trifasciata* (mother-in-law's tongue)
* *Schlumbergera truncata* (Christmas cactus)
* *Spathiphyllum wallisii* (peace lily)

TIP
Lavender oil is a traditional sleeping aid, but rather than splashing the cash on lavender pillow sprays and lavender-filled eye masks – lovely as they are – why not introduce a lavender plant into your bedroom instead?

This page:
A line-up of hanging planters is an imaginative way of displaying plants in a bedroom, shown here with *Rhipsalis baccifera* (mistletoe cactus), *Tradescantia* (wandering Jew) and *Epipremnum aureum* (devil's ivy).

This page:
A floor-standing plant, like this *Dracaena fragrans* (Deremensis Group) 'Warneckei' (striped dracaena), in an attractive container makes a welcoming addition to a guest bedroom.

This page:
A line-up of tiny, trailing
Hedera helix (English ivy),
hanging down from pots
grouped on the bed head,
turns a plain bedside
shelf into a striking
design statement.

BEDSIDE TABLES

Whether your bedside table is a beautiful piece of furniture or a stack of vintage suitcases, it is essentially a practical space for keeping useful paraphernalia to hand such as reading material, a table lamp and an alarm clock. Given that there isn't much surface area to play with – and we are not in favour of style over substance or usefulness – any plant placed on a bedside table has the simple role of upgrading its look, particularly if it's in a lovely pot, and it has to be neat and compact.

If, however, there really is no space for a plant, no matter how small, you could attach a small ledge or shelf behind the table for a line-up of individually potted teeny plants such as miniature *Hedera helix* 'Sagittifolia' (English ivy) or *Aloe vera* (Barbados aloe). Placing a plant on the bedside table in a guest bedroom is a welcoming gesture.

NEAT PLANTS FOR BEDSIDE TABLES

* *Aeonium tabulaeforme* (flat-topped aeonium)
* *Asplenium nidus* (bird's nest fern)
* *Dendrobium* orchids
* *Kalanchoe blossfeldiana* (flaming Katy)
* *Lavandula* (lavender)

Below:
The compact growth of *Sansevieria trifasciata* (mother-in-law's tongue) makes it perfect for sitting on a bedside table where there is little space to spare.

Below right:
A tray-based hanging planter is a novel way to showcase a selection of plants, like this collection of ferns and a *Maranta leuconeura* var. *erythroneura* (herringbone plant).

This page:
Cattleya and *Phalaenopsis* orchids are night-time oxygenators, improving the quality of the air we breathe as we sleep, which makes them a healthy choice for a bedside table.

The top of a wardrobe or bedroom cupboard is ideal for displaying plants. More often than not, this is a dead space and so an effective piece of plant landscaping will have lots of impact. It is also safely out of the way, so it's the perfect place for plants that are not particularly child- or pet-friendly.

The space on top of a cupboard actually gives you lots of scope for experimenting with your plant styling – from a single statement flower to a straightforward line-up of the same type of plants, a small mixed grouping to a full-on indoor border of bushy, medium-sized and trailing plants.

Looking up isn't just about the tops of cupboards. Run laterally with the idea and you could find yourself adding an indoor tree. Because it is unexpected, the effect will be really arresting. A *Dracaena fragrans* 'Janet Craig' or *D. fragrans* 'Massangeana' (corn plant) are always a good choice, for their narrow spread and toxin-filtering properties. Other 'tree-like' plants that would also work well include *Yucca elephantipes* (spineless yucca) and *Ficus cyathistipula*.

A single macramé pot holder hanging from the ceiling can be surprisingly effective, as can a simple grouping or line-up of three individual planters hung at slightly different heights. Alternatively, opt for one large planter that can hold a couple or more plants – think of it as an indoor hanging basket.

LOOKING UP

Left:
Displaying a trailing *Scindapsus pictus* (silver vine), an assortment of ferns and *Rhipsalis paradoxa* (chain cactus) in the dead space on top of a cupboard creates a lovely indoor 'border'.

Above:
A vintage suitcase, out of harm's way on top of a cabinet, makes an innovative container for a selection of ferns and a *Rhipsalis paradoxa* (chain cactus).

WARDROBE 'BORDER' PLANTS
Aglaonema 'Silver Queen' (Chinese evergreen)
Asparagus setaceus (asparagus fern)
Philodendron scandens (heart-leaf philodendron)
Platycerium bifurcatum (staghorn fern)
Rhipsalis paradoxa (chain cactus)

OTHER SURFACES

Above:
Different plants are given coherence when planted in the same type of pot: cactus, *Asplenium nidus* (bird's nest fern) and *Tradescantia cerinthoides* 'Variegata' (flowering inch plant).

Below:
Beaucarnea recurvata (elephant's foot) and *Guzmania* in their sparkly containers introduce colour and interest into a practical dressing room.

Whether the style of your bedroom is boutique hotel chic, industrial luxe, mid-century retro, pared-back minimalist or modern country, there will be a plant – and a container – to suit it.

As with other rooms in the house, you need to view all surfaces and furniture as planting opportunities, from windowsills and mantelpieces to chests of drawers and dressing tables. Landscape your chosen surface with a mix of decorative items and plants for a co-ordinated still-life effect. Less is often more with these types of display, and a carefully chosen plant that fits in with the *objet*s and look of the space can have real impact – like a *Scindapsus pictus* (silver vine) or pink-tinged *Tradescantia zebrina* (silver inch plant) trailing down the side of a chest of drawers. Flowering plants can be used to introduce a jolt of unexpected colour into the room: a single, bold, architectural *Guzmania lingulata* (scarlet star plant) or *Hippeastrum* (amaryllis) standing to attention is particularly striking.

A terrarium can be neatly tucked onto the side of a dressing table or chest of drawers, while a larger vessel can be planted up with a grouping of the same plants and even positioned on the floor. If you have a set of shelves, create a mini vertical garden, leading the eye from bottom to top with bits of mixed planting dotted in between any books, picture frames and ornaments.

CLEAN-AIR STATEMENT PLANTS
* *Beaucarnea recurvata* (elephant's foot)
* *Chamaedorea seifrizii* (bamboo palm)
* *Chlorophytum comosum* (spider plant)
* *Dracaena fragrans* 'Janet Craig' (corn plant)
* *Dypsis lutescens* (bamboo palm)
* *Epipremnum aureum* (devil's ivy)
* *Ficus benjamina* (weeping fig)
* *Hedera helix* (English ivy)
* *Nephrolepis exaltata* 'Bostoniensis' (Boston fern)
* *Schefflera actinophylla* (Queensland umbrella plant)

This page:
The subtly pink tips of
a *Tradescantia cerinthoides*
'Variegata' (flowering
inch plant) give a gentle
lift to the neutral tones
used in this bedroom.

12
PLANTS FOR SLEEPING SPACES

Stephanotis floribunda
Common name:
Madagascar jasmine
Light: Good light, but
not direct sunlight
Care: High humidity,
keep moist; reduce water
over winter
Tips: Keep cool in
winter and ensure high
humidity from spring
to promote flowering

Aloe vera
Common name:
Barbados aloe
Light: Bright light
Care: Keep compost moist
Tips: Easy to grow and care
for, but avoid fluctuations
in temperature

Phalaenopsis
Common name:
Moth orchid
Light: Place in good light,
but not direct sunlight
Care: Tolerates high
humidity; allow surface to
dry out between waterings
Tips: Cut stem back to
second notch from the
base after flowering to
encourage future flowers

Platycerium bifurcatum
Common name:
Staghorn fern
Light: Low to medium
light
Care: Moderate moisture
Tips: Mist daily

Chlorophytum comosum
Common name:
Spider plant
Light: Bright to moderate light
Care: Keep compost moist
Tips: Easy to grow and easy to propagate – snip off the 'babies' and plant on

Gardenia jasminoides
Common name:
Cape jasmine
Light: Bright light, but not direct sun
Care: Tolerates high humidity; keep compost moist but do not over-water
Tips: Beautifully scented, but can be sensitive and difficult to get to re-flower

Gerbera jamesonii
Common name:
Barberton daisy
Light: Good light
Care: Keep compost moist while in bloom; can dry out slightly afterwards
Tips: Remove dead flowers to encourage blooming for as long as possible

Hedera helix
Common name:
English ivy
Light: Bright light
Care: Allow surface of compost to dry between waterings
Tips: A great trailing plant that can be trained into different shapes; keep well pruned

Sansevieria trifasciata
Common name:
Mother-in-law's tongue
Light: Good light
Care: Low watering requirements
Tips: One of the easiest houseplants to look after! Keep leaves clean

Epipremnum aureum
Common name:
Devil's ivy
Light: Moderate to bright light
Care: Moderate watering; tolerates dryness
Tips: Prune twice a year to keep the plant looking bushy and full

Spathiphyllum wallisii
Common name:
Peace lily
Light: Good light; can tolerate shade
Care: Keep compost moist; thrives in higher humidity
Tips: Remove flowering stems when the blooms ripen to green; keep leaves clean and polished

Syngonium podophyllum
Common name:
Arrowhead vine
Light: Moderate light
Care: Keep compost slightly moist

BATHING SPACES

We have to walk a bit of a tightrope when designing and decorating our bathrooms. While their main purpose is to be a practical space, they are also a haven, where we undertake the soothing rituals of cleansing and beautifying ourselves.

Most bathrooms tend to fall into one of two camps: light and humid, or dark and humid. While light levels are obviously a key consideration when choosing plants for any space, with a bathroom you need to select humidity-loving plants above all. This means that cacti and most succulents are an absolute no-no. Instead, aim your sights at plants like orchids, ferns and palms, which all like humidity and can also tolerate fluctuations in temperature.

Aloes are commonly associated with bathrooms – perhaps because they are a natural antiseptic – while the *Saintpaulia* (African violet)

HUMIDITY-LOVING PLANTS
* Ferns, such as *Nephrolepis exaltata* 'Bostoniensis' (Boston fern) and *Asparagus setaceus* (asparagus fern)
* *Guzmania lingulata* (scarlet star plant)
* *Saintpaulia* (African violet)
* *Spathiphyllum wallisii* (peace lily)

is more than happy with the typically damp and humid conditions. Conveniently, there is a rather cute micro-miniature variety, which is perfect for a small spot.

Ferns had their heyday during the Victorian era but they are now having a bit of a style resurgence. As well as being perfect bathroom plants, thriving in damp conditions with low light levels, they also look pretty dramatic, too. Try a bold *Asplenium nidus* (bird's nest fern), a showy *Nephrolepis exaltata* 'Fluffy Ruffles' (sword fern) or an impressive *Platycerium bifurcatum* (staghorn fern).

When there is the space, bathrooms can lend themselves to some pretty spectacular planting: a pair of tall *Howea forsteriana* (Kentia palm) bookending a roll-top bath look glorious, as does a 'living curtain' of *Vanda* orchids draping down in front of a window.

How you use your bathroom will help you decide where to position the plants. A good starting point is to have plants within your sightline when taking a long, relaxing soak in the tub or an invigorating power shower. Even if your bathroom is spatially challenged, there is always room to introduce plants: just choose miniature

TIP
Foliage plants are a better choice for a bathroom that's on the dark side than flowering plants, which generally need higher levels of light.

This page:
A spacious bathroom
allows for an interesting
variety of humidity-
loving plants. From left:
Tradescantia (wandering
Jew); *Hedera helix* (English
ivy); *Nephrolepis exaltata*
(sword fern); *Schefflera*
(umbrella tree) and
Peperomia scandens
'Variegata' (variegated
Cupid peperomia).

DR ALOE VERA

The sap from *Aloe vera* (Barbados aloe) is brilliant at treating a number of skin ailments, such as sunburn, eczema and insect bites. If you grow one of these living pharmacies, here's how you should use the sap. Remember that it is only effective when used fresh.

✳ For treating just a small wound, break off a little, unobtrusive leaf or a small part of a leaf and gently rub the broken end onto the affected area.

✳ If the problem is larger, break off a whole leaf and let the sap drip from the bottom into a small container. Once the dripping has finished, rub the sap onto the wound with your fingers.

✳ If you need more sap, carefully cut the leaf open to extract any that's left inside.

varieties and dot them in among your lotions and potions, or select plants that are slow-growing or happy with a robust pruning come spring.

Occasionally, within the layout of a home, the bathroom is slotted into an internal, windowless space. If this is the case with yours, then you will just have to forget about using any plants here – no plant, no matter how resilient it is, can survive without any access to natural light.

Above:
Aglaonema 'Silver Queen' (Chinese evergreen) makes an ideal bathroom plant, thriving in the moist air and tolerating shade.

Right:
A mature *Ficus lyrata* (fiddle-leaf fig) is a dramatic-enough plant to make a strong statement all by itself.

Left:
The healing properties of
Aloe vera (Barbados aloe)
give the plant a natural
affinity with bathrooms.

Below left:
When choosing bathroom
plants, look out for
varieties that do well in a
moist environment.

Just one well-chosen plant will create impact in a bathroom – think of a tall, narrow *Howea forsteriana* (Kentia palm) tucked into a corner, an effusive *Nephrolepis exaltata* 'Bostoniensis' (Boston fern) hanging down over one end of the bathtub or a repetitive line-up of spiky, architectural *Aloe humilis* (spider aloe) along a windowsill.

If the bathtub is freestanding, a useful little table or storage unit placed next to it could benefit from a small version of a plant such as a *Schefflera actinophylla* (Queensland umbrella plant) placed on top. If the tub is fitted, then banish the lotions and potions from one corner and replace them with a plant – just avoid bushy or trailing numbers for this kind of position. Meanwhile, a neatly potted *Haworthia margaritifera* (pearl-bearer) on one corner of a sink shelf or, even better, a matching pair on each end, creates a lot of impact for a small plant.

While coloured fixtures and patterned tiling are making a comeback in bathroom design, most of us still plump for timeless white fittings. In planting terms, this is a good thing. The rich, vibrant greens of foliage plants that suit a bathroom environment really sing out against a light-reflecting white backdrop.

BATH & SINK SURROUNDS

FOCAL POINT BATHROOM PLANTS
* *Asplenium nidus* (bird's nest fern)
* *Hedera helix* (English ivy)
* *Oncidium* orchids
* *Sansevieria trifasciata* (mother-in-law's tongue)
* *Spathiphyllum wallisii* (peace lily)

This page:
Ferns, such as *Asplenium nidus*
(bird's nest fern), are a
good choice for a bathroom
that has little natural light.

This page:
A pair of humidity-loving *Howea forsteriana* (Kentia palm), placed at either end of a roll-top bath, makes for a truly show-stopping display. An *Asplenium nidus* (bird's nest fern) and *Adiantum raddianum* (Delta maidenhair fern) complete the look.

Left:
A selection of miniature succulents and *Hedera helix* (English ivy), all in white containers, add interest to this in-built bathroom storage. The plants will need to be swapped around every two weeks so those on the lower shelf receive their share of natural light.

Below:
Philodendron scandens (heart-leaf philodendron) drapes gently down this bathroom cabinet, softening its hard, angular edges.

SOFTENING HARD LINES

Whether we want it to happen or not, bathrooms can often end up looking or feeling quite clinical and therefore 'hard'. This is generally down to the typical materials used in bathroom design – namely, ceramic, stone, metal and glass, not to mention tiles and mirrors. But plants can soften this impression. Choose those that will waft and move in any slight breeze or draught. Loose, trailing varieties such as *Epipremnum aureum* (devil's ivy), *Peperomia scandens Variegata* (Cupid peperomia) and *Tradescantia* (wandering Jew) work especially well, draped over shelf edges, tucked into in-built niches or displayed in a hanging planter.

Another benefit of plants is that they are really good at reducing noise by absorbing, diffracting and deflecting sound waves, which is particularly useful in rooms with hard surfaces, such as the bathroom. Positioning plants in a corner or creating a grouping at different heights – try a *Dracaena fragrans* 'Massangeana' (corn plant) and a *Philodendron bipinnatifidum* (horsehead philodendron) – will give you the maximum noise reduction, and that tinny echo that currently rattles around the space will be a thing of the past.

FIVE GREAT NOISE ABSORBERS
* *Dracaena draco* (dragon tree)
* *Ficus benjamina* (weeping fig)
* *Philodendron bipinnatifidum* (horsehead philodendron)
* *Schefflera arboricola* (umbrella tree)
* *Spathiphyllum wallisii* (peace lily)

TRAILING PLANTS FOR BATHROOMS
* *Chlorophytum comosum* (spider plant)
* *Epipremnum aureum* (devil's ivy)
* *Hedera helix* (English ivy)
* *Philodendron scandens* (heart-leaf philodendron)
* *Tetrastigma voinierianum* (chestnut vine)

Above left:
Vanda orchids love the warm, damp conditions of the bathroom and look incredibly dramatic suspended from wires, with their roots on display.

Above right:
Both *Tradescantia* (wandering Jew) and *Aloe vera* (Barbados aloe), thrive in the damp and humid conditions typical of bathrooms.

OTHER IDEAS

Orchids are particularly fond of the hot, humid conditions in a bathroom and can be a dramatic and colourful addition. *Phalaenopsis* species (moth orchids) are pretty indestructible and widely available, but Ian's current favourites are *Vanda* orchids, which behave like air plants and happily survive unpotted. And the requirement to mist their roots every day will happen anyway in a well-used family bathroom. Because they are so extraordinary, just one can have a huge impact.

Plants with coloured or variegated foliage are another good way to introduce an additional design detail into a bright bathroom. Try an *Aglaonema* 'Silver Queen' (Chinese evergreen) or a *Calathea makoyana* (peacock plant).

Choose containers to highlight any accent colours or finishes and to complement or contrast with the bathroom fittings. Use metallic pots to emphasize any brassware, or introduce a monochrome theme with black planters if the room is totally white. White ceramic pots are the default neutral choice for a bathroom – select these if you want your plants to do the talking.

Bathrooms often have limited floor space, so you will probably need to look up when positioning plants – think shelves or the tops of cupboards and cabinets. A display of hanging planters dangling over the bathtub works very well but make sure they don't hang too low or you will risk banging your head every time you get in and out of the tub.

12
PLANTS FOR BATHING SPACES

Phalaenopsis
Common name: Moth orchid
Light: Place in good light, but not direct sunlight
Care: Tolerates high humidity
Tips: Cut stem back to second notch from the base after flowering to encourage future flowers

Aloe vera
Common name: Barbados aloe
Light: Bright light
Care: Keep compost moist
Tips: Easy to grow and care for, but avoid fluctuations in temperature

Dionaea muscipula
Common name: Venus fly trap
Light: Good light, avoid direct sun
Care: Never allow to dry out
Tips: Use distilled water; ideal for terrariums

Hedera helix
Common name: English ivy
Light: Bright light
Care: Allow surface of compost to dry between waterings
Tips: A great trailing plant that can be trained into different shapes; keep well pruned

Aphelandra squarrosa
Common name:
Zebra plant
Light: Bright light
Care: Keep compost moist
Tips: Clip off flower branch after a few days to encourage future blooms

Aspenium nidus
Common name:
Bird's nest fern
Light: Moderate light; avoid direct sun
Care: Water lightly and often
Tips: Clip off brown fronds with scissors

Chamaedorea elegans
Common name:
Parlour palm
Light: Low light
Care: Always keep moist
Tips: Mist regularly to increase humidity

Chlorophytum comosum
Common name:
Spider plant
Light: Bright to moderate light
Care: Keep compost moist
Tips: Easy to grow and easy to propagate – snip off the 'babies' and plant on

Medinilla magnifica
Common name:
Rose grape
Light: Bright filtered light
Care: Enjoys high humidity; water moderately
Tips: Prune the plant back to half its size after flowering to promote future blossoms

Philodendron xanadu
Common name:
None
Light: Moderate light
Care: Allow to dry out between waterings
Tips: Tuck aerial roots back into the pot

Spathiphyllum wallisii
Common name:
Peace lily
Light: Likes good light, but can tolerate shade
Care: Thrives in higher humidity; keep compost moist
Tips: Remove flowering stems when the blooms ripen to green; keep leaves clean and polished

Vanda orchid
Common name:
None
Light: Good light; avoid direct sun
Care: Tolerates high humidity
Tips: Mist daily and avoid roots becoming soggy

CHILDREN'S SPACES

It's good to teach young children how to nurture a living thing. They enjoy getting their hands dirty, and doing some indoor gardening lets them see how nature works in close-up. Choose plants for them that are easy to grow and look after, such as succulents and *Kalanchoe blossfeldiana* (flaming Katy). Alternatively, start them off with plants that grow quickly, such as cress (see page 125).

Encourage young children to grow plants from the seeds they find in some of the fruit or veg you eat, such as apples, chillies or avocadoes. You won't get any sort of meaningful crop, but it's enjoyable to do. See pages 22-3 for other edibles that are easy to grow indoors.

Chlorophytum comosum (spider plant), which sprouts 'babies' at a rate of knots, and *Maranta leuconeura* (prayer plant), which folds its leaves at night, are fun choices for young children, too, and they also grow quickly and easily. Let them plant a container of small spring bulbs – try *Muscari* (grape hyacinth), *Galanthus* (snowdrop) or *Crocus* – and watch them develop and bloom.

TIP

···········

Remember to teach children good gardening hygiene: never to taste or eat any part of a plant (apart from any edibles, of course!) and always wash their hands after doing any gardening.

Above:
Fun planting containers add extra appeal, such as this Lego storage head, filled with *Beaucarnea recurvata* (elephant's foot).

Right:
A terrarium becomes even more fun when accessorized with favourite small toys, such as these Schleich animals.

THE CIRCUS AND OTHER STORIES

YOUNGER CHILDREN

Miniature gardens and small, trough-style containers with a mixed selection of easy-to-grow plants, such as *Beaucarnea recurvata* (elephant's foot) and *Crassula ovata* (money tree), are perfect contained plantings for younger children to look after. The same goes for miniaturized versions of 'grown-up' plants, such as *Asparagus setaceus* (asparagus fern), *Ficus microcarpa* 'Ginseng' (Indian laurel) and *Hypoestes phyllostachya* (polka dot plant), which are particularly cute in their smaller forms.

Have fun with the plant containers, too. Try out Lego storage heads and other pieces of children's paraphernalia, such as pencil pots, melamine cups, sweet tins and so on. There are a plethora of quirky, cute, kitsch and humorous pots on the market – whether brightly decorated, with faces on, or in the shapes of animals – which all slot extremely well into children's rooms. A lovely but also rather effective idea is to incorporate a few small toys, figurines or models alongside the plants, to capture the child's imagination.

Safety is, of course, a key consideration when introducing plants into a younger child's room. Obviously, avoid spiky cacti as well as plants that are potentially toxic if ingested, such as *Spathiphyllum wallisii* (peace lily), *Sansevieria trifasciata* (mother-in-law's tongue) and *Epipremnum aureum* (devil's ivy). Think carefully, too, about where to position them so they are out of reach or tucked away where they won't be easily knocked over.

Left:
Intersperse the paraphernalia on a child's shelf with some easy-care plants.

Above:
A white wicker basket is given a colour boost with spiky *Guzmania* and dramatic *Medinilla magnifica* (rose grape).

TIP
....
With very young children, use planters made from plastic or metal – rather than ceramic or terracotta – as they are both lighter and more robust when being handled.

GROWING CRESS
A classic project for a young child. Even more exciting if you use a container with a face, so you are effectively growing its hair.
* Place some soggy kitchen paper in your pot of choice.
* Sprinkle over the cress seeds and put in a shady spot.
* When they begin to sprout, move to a light windowsill. The cress will be ready to harvest after a week or so.

Right:
A neat line-up of
different-shaped cacti
planted in sophisticated
containers works well on
an older child's desk.

Opposite page:
Sansevieria cylindrica and
Asparagus setaceus (asparagus
fern) are handsome and
virtually indestructible
– useful qualities in a
teenager's room.

OLDER CHILDREN

When children grow up and turn from tweenagers into teenagers, having their own space becomes more and more important to them. As a parent, you need to make sure that you don't stifle their attempts at self-expression by trying to impose your taste on them. Instead, you need to work with them.

Tweens and teens tend to gravitate towards things that feel a bit more grown-up and edgy. In plant terms, this translates into all the varieties that have something quirky about them, even verging on the macabre. Think of those plants that have a bit of a story to tell: for example, *Tillandsia* (air plant), any number of cool-looking cacti or the various members of the fern family, which date back to prehistoric times.

By this age, your child is likely to have accumulated quite a lot of stuff, so a good approach is to choose plants that can be dotted in among their books and bits and pieces. This is generation smartphone, and older children are well versed in what looks good. Photogenic shelfie-style arrangements will appeal to this crowd.

Plants with variegated or colourful foliage, such as *Maranta leuconeura* var. *erythroneura* (herringbone plant) and *Begonia rex* (fan plant), can be used as a subtle way of introducing colour into an older child's room. Flowering plants will probably appeal more if they are peculiar or idiosyncratic in some way: the bromeliads, for example, such as *Guzmania lingulata* (scarlet star plant) and *Vriesea splendens* (flaming sword), will work a treat. If something bolder is wanted, consider a larger specimen plant, such as an architectural *Howea forsteriana* (Kentia palm). The added bonus of all these plants is that they are pretty sturdy and good-looking.

TIP
....
Succulents are
brilliant starter plants
for children of all ages.
Compact in size, they can
take a fair amount of neglect,
if, for example, they are
accidentally left unwatered
for a few weeks.

Left:
Cacti that can cope with missing the odd watering now and then are always a good choice for an older child's bedroom.

Right:
Displayed like an animal skull, a prehistoric-looking *Tillandsia* (air plant) often appeals to teenagers because of its unusual, somewhat quirky, nature.

QUIRKY PLANTS FOR OLDER KIDS

✳ *Codiaeum variegatum* var. *pictum* (croton). The different hybrids have dramatically vibrant foliage with variously shaped leaves. They need a bit of care, so these are best for your budding horticulturist.

✳ Desert cacti. The sheer variety of shapes and sizes, and the fact they are pretty much unkillable, gives them an edge.

✳ *Dionaea muscipula* (Venus fly trap). These are the spectacular-looking carnivores of the plant world.

✳ *Lithops* (living stone). As well as really looking like small stones, these produce surprising, dramatic flowers in autumn.

✳ *Tillandsia* (air plant). These plants are amazing because of their quirk of quite literally living on air.

As for containers and where to position them, the same rules apply here as to everywhere else in the home, but let your child take the lead. Would they like subtle, sophisticated planters or prefer something a little more colourful and unusual? Do they want to position the plant in a spot that commands immediate attention or would they prefer smaller varieties that can be subtly accommodated among their other possessions? Are they keen on the idea of an on-trend terrarium?

As teenagers have a tendency to be a bit on the clumsy side, make sure their plants are placed on a stable surface or tucked safely out of the way of any accidental knocks: think towards the back of a shelf or desk, rather than at the front, or, if they are standing on the floor, positioned in a corner.

Above all, be realistic, it's probably best to choose varieties of plants that can take a fair bit of neglect in case the 'Keep Out' sign goes on the door and you aren't allowed access to water any plants for a few weeks at a time…

TIP
....
Why not get your older child to design and plant up a terrarium scheme? The following plants are all good choices: *Crassula ovata* (money tree), *Tillandsia* (air plant) and the various small forms of fern, cacti and succulents.

12
PLANTS FOR CHILDREN'S SPACES

Gerbera jamesonii
Common name: Barberton daisy
Light: Good light
Care: Keep moist while in bloom; can dry out slightly afterwards
Tips: Remove dead flowers to encourage blooming for as long as possible

Codiaeum variegatum
Common name: Croton/ Joseph's coat
Light: Good light
Care: Keep slightly moist
Tips: Prune top when plant becomes tall, and root like a stem tip cutting

Maranta leuconeura
Common name: Prayer plant
Light: Moderate light
Care: Enjoys high humidity; keep compost moist
Tips: Trim back to keep shape and promote new growth

Philodendron xanadu
Common name: None
Light: Moderate light
Care: Allow to dry out between waterings
Tips: Tuck aerial roots back into the pot

Dionaea muscipula
Common name:
Venus fly trap
Light: Good light;
avoid direct sun
Care: Keep moist,
but don't over-water
Tips: Use distilled water;
ideal for terrariums

Echeveria elegans
Common name:
Mexican gem
Light: Bright light
Care: Keep slightly moist
Tips: Cut off the offshoots
and propagate them to
prevent the pot from
becoming overcrowded

Kalanchoe blossfeldiana
Common name:
Flaming Katy
Light: Place in good light,
but not in direct sunlight
Care: Water only when
compost is dry
Tips: Pinch off blooms
after the flowers fade to
preserve look of the plant

Lithops
Common name:
Living stone
Light: Good light
Care: Water lightly in
spring and autumn
Tips: Keep dry in summer
and winter to follow
natural growth cycle

Schlumbergera truncata
Common name:
Christmas cactus
Light: Place in
indirect light
Care: Needs well-
drained compost;
tolerates high humidity
Tips: Avoid over-watering,
under-watering or other
stress to prevent flowers
from dropping

Tillandsia cyanea
Common name:
Pink quill
Light: Bright light
Care: Spray twice weekly;
keep moist
Tips: Keep cool in
winter to encourage
spring blooms

Tradescantia fluminensis
Common name:
Wandering Jew
Light: Bright to
moderate light
Care: Water thoroughly;
allow surface of compost to
dry out between waterings
Tips: Small pink flowers
appear in spring

Vanda orchid
Common name:
None
Light: Good light;
avoid direct sun
Care: Tolerates high
humidity; mist daily
Tips: Avoid roots
becoming soggy

WORKING SPACES

More and more of us are spending at least some part of our working lives doing our jobs from home – whether full-time, part-time or the odd day here and there. This means that an office is now a more frequent feature of our homes than ever before. It can be as simple and straightforward as a desk tucked into a discreet corner of the house or a full-on, fully equipped room, complete with reference library and all the current techy mod cons.

Since a home office is a working space, it obviously needs to be practical with all the resources you need for the job in hand easily accessible, but it should also be inspirational – somewhere that pushes you to be creative and to do your best work. With that in mind, what could be more pleasant than looking up from your computer for a screen break and finding your eyes alighting on some carefully chosen plants?

Colour theory classifies green as the colour of nature, which isn't exactly rocket science, especially as we are talking about plants! However, it is the anecdotal associations given to the colour that are interesting in this context.

Green is perceived as the colour of calm and it is believed to relieve stress – just what you need when under pressure from a work deadline. It is also considered to be the colour of stability and endurance – keep plugging away at that project. Historically, it has been associated with wisdom, intelligence and confidence – all qualities we would like in our working selves.

People also associate green with good health, so it's interesting that as well as there being all the positive mood benefits linked with the colour green, plants in an office will bring actual health benefits – but more about that over the page.

So, what more excuses do you need? Start greening up your home office now.

TIP

Houseplants are much more than eye candy. There are a number of positive psychological reasons for introducing some greenery into an office zone.

GREEN PSYCHOLOGY

In the world of psychology, the colour green makes you feel:

* Positive
* Calm
* Relaxed
* Uplifted
* Refreshed

* Stable
* Clever
* Confident
* Tranquil
* Balanced

This page:
Choose smaller varieties of
your preferred plants for
a desktop scheme, such as
this collection of ferns.

This page:
Dotting small succulents
and cacti among reference
books and stationery adds
visual interest without
taking up too much space.

Left:
A stationery trolley makes a portable plant container. Here, *Spathiphyllum wallisii* (peace lily), known for its pollutant-filtering properties, has been added to a mixed planting scheme.

Below:
A 'living wall'-style planter is space-saving and an interesting way of introducing planting into a small office. This one is planted with a mixture of ferns and succulents.

HEALTH

We discussed the health benefits of having plants in the home earlier in the book (see page 14), but let's explore it a bit more here in the context of an office space. As most research has focused on the benefits of having indoor plants in large corporate offices, it stands to reason that many of their findings also apply to a domestic office space.

Ian and the team at Indoor Garden Design

TIP
....
Adding plants to your office as air filters makes sense in terms of your health as well as aesthetically.

have collated many of the research papers that have investigated the positive effects of plants in an office environment and have concluded that introducing just one plant near your work station can start to bring about positive effects. It will reduce feelings of anxiety and stress and also help to improve concentration – particularly for those of us whose work is computer-based.

An especially significant study done in 2009 at the University of Technology in Sydney, Australia, came to the conclusion that it is highly probable that all plants absorb toxins from the air as part of their biological processes. The kinds of toxins we are talking about are those pesky volatile organic compounds (VOCs) – see also page 14. In essence these are the invisible pollutants released from the many common man-made products that we all have in our homes, such as carpets and cleaning products. If we have a home office, then there are the additional VOCs from computers, printers and other common office essentials.

My Dad has always been convinced that the humble spider plant (*Chlorophytum comosum*) is a good absorber of computer 'emissions'. The rest of the family dismissed the theory, but it turns out he has a point – *Chlorophytum* plants are particularly good at processing environmental pollutants.

HEALTHY HOME OFFICE PLANTS
* *Aglaonema modestum* (Chinese evergreen)
* *Anthurium scherzerianum* (flamingo flower)
* *Chlorophytum comosum* (spider plant)
* *Dracaena fragrans* 'Janet Craig' (corn plant)
* *Epipremnum aureum* (devil's ivy)
* *Ficus benjamina* (weeping fig)
* *Philodendron scandens* (heart-leaf philodendron)
* *Spathiphyllum wallisii* (peace lily)

DESKS

A desk is usually the main focus of an office zone, where you sit to work and where, no doubt, your computer is set up. It also offers another surface with planting potential. As you will see the plants on your desk in close-up, small in this situation really is beautiful. A couple of well-chosen *Aloe* and *Echeveria* dotted among your stationery, or a trailing *Epipremnum aureum* (devil's ivy) spilling over the side edge of the desk, will create the sense of an effective planting. And since desk space is likely to be at a premium, succulents are generally an appropriate choice because they are slow-growing.

Be inventive with your plant containers, perhaps using an old desk tidy, some pen pots or a wastepaper basket. Look out for containers with finishes in light-industrial materials such as galvanized zinc, enamel or mesh, or create your own DIY pots wrapped in brown paper, string or newspaper for a quirky touch.

Whichever look you go for, just make sure that the container is waterproof or can be made to be so – the last thing you need is an accidental leak onto your work or computer. If you tend to be a little clumsy, a group planting in a self-contained trough or planter works well. However, individually potted plants give you the flexibility to move them out of the way whenever you need a bit more desk space.

Home office desks are often positioned in front of, or close to, a window, so you will need to take that into account when selecting your plants, making sure they can cope with the amount of light and its intensity.

Some of the design tricks covered elsewhere in the book can also be called upon for the desk. Neat line-ups of the same plant variety work well, as does a display that focuses on foliage colours or the intricate shapes of small plant specimens, such as the various cacti or *Aloe*, because you will look at them in close-up. Last, but by no means least, the trusty terrarium is a very useful, tidy and compact solution for a desk-friendly design.

Above:
A self-contained trough ensures that a group planting, like this collection of *Beaucarnea recurvata* (elephant's foot), doesn't take up too much space on a desk.

Right:
Place a restful green display in your line of sight. *Sansevieria trifasciata* var. *laurentii* (variegated snake plant) is compact, slow-growing and tolerant of all degrees of light, shade and heat.

TINY PLANTS FOR CLOSE-UPS

* *Aloe variegata* (partridge breast aloe)
* *Crassula muscosa* 'Variegata'
* *Echeveria secunda* var. *glauca* (glaucous echeveria)
* *Echinopsis rhodotricha* (a type of cactus)
* *Tillandsia* (air plant)

Far left:
Bushy and trailing plants
look particularly good
when displayed on a
shelving unit.

Left:
Use individually potted
plants as spacers in order
to break up solid rows of
reference books.

SHELVES & OTHER SPACES

HIDING A HOME OFFICE

If your home office is part of a larger space,
you can screen it off from the rest of the room
with a line-up of tall plants. *Howea forsteriana*
(Kentia palm), *Dracaena fragrans* (corn plant),
Yucca elephantipes (spineless yucca), or, if it is a
bright room, *Ficus benjamina* (weeping fig) or
Euphorbia tirucalli (finger tree), all fit the bill
with their dramatic outlines, plus they have
the additional benefit of filtering pollutants
from the air.

Shelves, as we know, are very useful for displaying
plants. Such displays work best when they are
kept simple and bold: try using a few individually
potted plants as decorative spacers to break up
solid rows of reference and text books. You could
even employ a plant as a bookend.

If the shelves are deep enough, use the area
in front of the books to arrange a neat line-up
of plants. This is also a good way to camouflage
unattractive box folders or magazine files. Create
an indoor view with a grouped arrangement on a
shelf at eye level. For an effective bit of eye balm,
aim for the height you look at when looking up
from your computer screen. Trailing plants look
dramatic trailing over the edge of shelves and
particularly effective on a tall shelving unit.

No room on your desk for plants? Then be
bold and choose a tall, freestanding specimen
that can stand guard over you while you work.
Alternatively, put a plant stand, a stool or some
library steps to good use as a way of giving
medium-sized plants more presence. Employ
the top tray of a stationery trolley or soften the
functional lines of a filing cabinet by placing a
cluster of three *Sansevieria trifasciata* 'Hahnii' (bird's
nest sansevieria) or five different *Echeveria* on top.

If there just isn't a free flat surface in your
home office, it's still possible to introduce some
planting – with hanging planters. The trailing
plant varieties that look good draped over shelf
edges, such as *Trandescantia* (Wandering Jew) and
Rhipsalis baccifera (Mistletoe cactus), will also work
here. And there is nothing more fabulously
retro – and therefore chic – than a group of three
Chlorophytum comosum (spider plant) encased in
macramé pot holders hanging at different heights
over the corner of your desk.

12
PLANTS FOR WORKING SPACES

Howea forsteriana
Common name: Kentia palm
Light: Low light
Care: Keep moist
Tips: Relatively slow-growing; rarely needs repotting

Aechmea fasciata
Common name: Urn plant
Light: Bright light
Care: Lightly water roots; replenish water in its reservoir when it dries out
Tips: Epsom salts and bright light can be used to induce a pinkish orange bloom in spring

Crassula ovata
Common name: Money tree
Light: Needs plenty of light
Care: Tolerates high humidity; keep compost well drained
Tips: Plenty of light and fertilizer improves the leaf colour

Echeveria secunda
Common name: None
Light: Place in a bright spot
Care: Needs well-drained compost; tolerates medium humidity
Tips: Pinch off the blooms to preserve the appearance of the rosettes

Araucaria heterophylla
Common name: Norfolk Island palm
Light: High light levels
Care: Keep compost slightly moist
Tips: Turn the plant regularly to promote even growth; trim only lower branches, not from the top

Beaucarnea recurvata
Common name: Elephant's foot
Light: Bright light
Care: Enjoys high humidity; allow to dry out between waterings
Tips: Keep leaves clean with a damp cloth

Calathea makoyana
Common name: Peacock plant
Light: Bright light, but no direct sunlight
Care: Keep compost moist; enjoys high humidity
Tips: Mist daily

Chlorophytum comosum
Common name: Spider plant
Light: Bright to moderate light
Care: Keep slightly moist
Tips: Easy to grow and easy to propagate – snip off the 'babies' and plant on

Euphorbia tirucalli
Common name: Finger tree
Light: Full sunlight
Care: Water 3 times weekly over summer; keep compost well drained
Tips: Needs very little care; prune if it becomes too big

Ficus microcarpa 'Ginseng'
Common name: Indian laurel
Light: Bright, indirect light
Care: Keep moist
Tips: Prune regularly to retain the plant's shape; prune back to 2 leaves after 6–8 have grown

Monstera deliciosa
Common name: Swiss cheese plant
Light: Moderate light; no direct sun
Care: Allow compost to dry out between waterings
Tips: Secure aerial roots close to the base in the compost

Spathiphyllum wallisii
Common name: Peace lily
Light: Enjoys good light, but can also tolerate shade
Care: Thrives in higher humidity; keep compost moist
Tips: Remove flowering stems when the blooms ripen to green; keep leaves clean and polished

CONNECTING SPACES

In design terms, the hallway and staircase are no longer afterthoughts, but rather the spaces where you can set the whole style tone of your home. With that in mind, these areas really lend themselves to interesting indoor planting. Your hallway is the link between the outdoors and the indoors, and it's where you greet your guests, which makes it a logical place to introduce some planting if you're intent on greening up your home.

It almost goes without saying that the key thing to remember is to choose plants that can cope with the decreased light levels usually found in hallways. It also helps if they can handle any draughts coming in through a front door, and you should really aim for plants that stay compact simply because they are suited so much better to a limited space. Harness plants such as *Sansevieria trifasciata* (mother-in-law's tongue), *Zamioculcas zamiifolia* (fern arum) and *Dracaena fragrans* 'Massangeana' (corn plant) to create a dramatic mood. Alternatively, if you prefer a slightly softer feel, try *Epipremnum aureum* (devil's ivy) or *Tolmiea menziesii* (piggyback plant).

The hallway is also a brilliant space to experiment with seasonal planting and colour. Try a container filled with *Cyclamen persicum* (Persian cyclamen), miniature *Ilex* (holly) and *Hedera* (ivy) plants, or even a line-up of tiny *Pinus* (pine) trees at Christmas. Meanwhile, a bowl of scented bulbs such as *Hyacinthus* (hyacinth), *Narcissus* or *Primula* (primrose) will, quite literally, bring spring into your home.

As for the question of where to position your plants, a series of one plant per pot per step on a flight of stairs is particularly eye-catching, while a neat grouping of three or five different-sized plants clustered on a hall table can be really effective. In a small space, symmetry can work extremely well, so try 'bookending' a pair of matching plants on either side of a console. If you have the room, place a low bench or table against the wall and use this as a stand for a line-up of plants with similar foliage.

It is especially important to turn any houseplants regularly to ensure they have even access to natural light – no matter how limited it is – so that they grow evenly and to encourage fullness of growth. You will also need to move the pots from time to time to clean around them. With these considerations in mind, choose lightweight planters – think wicker and plastic over ceramic and terracotta – for ease of use.

This page:
An informal line-up of attractive plants makes a hallway particularly welcoming. From left: *Aglaonema modestum* (Chinese evergreen), *Stromanthe sanguinea* 'Triostar', *Codiaeum variegatum* var. *pictum* 'Petra' (Joseph's coat), *Calathea makoyana* (peacock plant), *Dracaena fragrans* (Deremensis Group) 'Lemon Lime' and *Beaucarnea recurvata* (elephant's foot).

ROBUST HALL & STAIRCASE PLANTS

All these plants can take a bash, a draught and not much light.

✳ *Aglaonema modestum* (Chinese evergreen)

✳ *Aspidistra elatior* (cast-iron plant)

✳ *Beaucarnea recurvata* (elephant's foot)

✳ *Crassula ovata* (money tree)

✳ *Dracaena fragrans* (corn plant)

✳ *Howea forsteriana* (Kentia palm)

✳ *Platycerium bifurcatum* (staghorn fern)

✳ *Sansevieria trifasciata* (mother-in-law's tongue)

✳ *Soleirolia soleirolii* (mind-your-own-business)

✳ *Yucca elephantipes* (spineless yucca)

✳ *Zamioculcas zamiifolia* (fern arum)

Below left:
Putting a small plant like a fern somewhere unexpected, such as hanging from a coat hook, greatly increases its impact.

Below right:
The turn in a staircase is put to good use with the addition of a slim *Dracaena fragrans* (Deremensis Group) 'Yellow Stripe' (corn plant).

TIP
....
Zamioculcas zamiifolia (fern arum) and *Sansevieria trifasciata* (mother-in-law's tongue) are Ian's perfect plants for staircases – they are both unbelievably hardy, stay compact and can cope with the lack of light.

This page:
Compact, hardy and tolerant of low light levels, draughts and fluctuating temperatures, *Sansevieria bacularis* 'Mikado' is the no-brainer houseplant of choice for a hallway.

Below left:
A dramatic display of
hanging *Vanda* orchids
in this period hallway
is complemented by
a stairway line-up of
Zamioculcas zamiifolia
(fern arum).

Below right:
Give interest to the
side of a staircase with
some textural planting.
Here, *Platycerium bifurcatum*
(staghorn fern) and *Rhipsalis
baccifera* (mistletoe cactus)
drape down through the
spindles and a basket of
palms sits below.

STAIRCASES

The staircase is often a missed design opportunity.
It gets an enormous amount of traffic, so it seems
an oversight that we don't always make better use of
it for expressing our taste preferences.

While edge-to-edge carpeted stairs don't
easily lend themselves to planting schemes,
stairways with a central runner, or polished or
painted wooden stairs, are the perfect frameworks
for certain plants. Stairs painted in a fail-safe
modernist monochrome, whether black or white,
provide an excellent backdrop to what are often
the deep foliage hues of hallway-appropriate
plants. Think how green really sings when
positioned against these colours and you will
understand how well they off-set plants. Varieties
with strong foliage shades that would work in this
context include *Zamioculcas zamiifolia* (fern arum),
Sansevieria trifasciata (mother-in-law's tongue) and
Crassula ovata (money tree).

While a simple scheme of one plant per pot per
step – or alternate step, depending on the scale and
height of both the plant and the staircase – leading

This page:
This narrow planter nestled in against the stair spindles has been planted with *Beaucarnea recurvata* (elephant's foot), which will gently waft in any breeze. Individual pots of *Sansevieria trifasciata* var. *laurentii* (variegated snake plant) look very smart lined up one behind the other on the stairs.

as far up the flight as you wish is really effective, there are other ways to look at styling a stairway. Try placing some trailing plants such as *Rhipsalis baccifera* (mistletoe cactus), *Rhoicissus rhomboidea* (grape ivy) and *Tetrastigma voinierianum* (chestnut vine) alongside the spindles, so that you can get them to drape through the gaps. A narrow trough or planter set against the banister on a landing area can allow you to introduce several plants into a smaller space. Again, if the banister has spindles, you can add some trailing varieties to the mix to drop down over the edge.

You can also put the draping technique to good use on the narrow niches, ledges and windowsills that so often feature in a stairwell. Positioning some trailing plants so that they cascade over a ledge is an attractive design device that can make an interesting feature of an otherwise ignored spot. An alternative is to create a grouping of petite pots on a narrow windowsill with appropriately scaled plants – like most staircase ideas, it is simple, yet very effective. Another often

overlooked location is the angle of a top or half-landing. These corners can provide a really good setting for a plant, effectively both framing and protecting it.

Stairway-appropriate plants are often foliage-based, so if you would like to introduce some strong colours or patterns to the space, look to your planters. The kinds of repetitive, line-up schemes that work well on a staircase can look even punchier if you have the plants in interesting containers.

Above left:
This position is perfect for troughs planted with multiple *Codiaeum variegatum* (croton), as they need plenty of light to keep them looking their best.

Above right:
Positioning trailing plants, such as these *Hedera helix* (English ivy), so that they cascade over a ledge makes a feature of an otherwise ignored spot.

This page:
A landing corner at the top of the stairs both frames and protects a mature and attractively bushy *Ficus lyrata* (fiddle-leaf fig).

HALLWAYS

Hallways are usually narrow, requiring compact planting, but that doesn't mean they can't have any impact. A tall, thin, architectural plant such as a mature *Euphorbia tirucalli* (finger tree) or a *Dracaena fragrans* 'compacta' (dragon tree) can be truly striking. Always choose a pot that's in proportion to the space – the last thing you need in a restricted hallway is a huge urn that everyone constantly bumps into.

Although one bold plant is the straightforward option, an original touch is to pop a plant somewhere unexpected – in a neat hanging planter off a coat hook or dangling from a newel post or a picture rail, for example. A few tiny specimens dotted along the top of a tall cupboard or a radiator cover can also be fun. For the latter, choose plants like succulents and cacti that don't mind warm, dry air and variations in heat. And, rather than hanging a picture or a mirror, how about a wall planter instead? Have a horizontal or vertical line of single planters or buy a specialist design that will allow you to plant up a mini 'living wall' (see page 59). Add a 'green path' of the same type of plant at even intervals next to the wall (so it isn't a trip hazard), to draw the eye through the length of the space.

Console tables and shoe cupboards are a useful addition if your hallway is wide enough to take one – not only as a dumping ground for general family detritus, but as a planting surface. If possible, position your plants at the end that gets the most light coming through door panes or fan lights.

ADDING COLOUR TO A HALLWAY

If your hallway has reasonable light, then choose plants with vibrant foliage colours or strikingly exotic flowers such as:

* *Anthurium scherzerianum* (flamingo flower)
* *Calathea makoyana* (peacock plant)
* *Cardiaeum variegatum* var. *pictum* 'Petra' (Joseph's coat)
* *Guzmania lingulata* (scarlet star plant)
* *Vriesia splendens* (flaming sword)

Left:
Thin, tall and architectural, this *Euphorbia tirucalli* (finger tree) makes an eye-catching addition to a narrow hallway.

Above:
Take advantage of a console table as a display surface. This *Zamioculcas zamiifolia* (fern arum) and *Platycerium bifurcatum* (staghorn fern) both cope well with the lower light levels often found in hallways.

12
PLANTS FOR CONNECTING SPACES

Aglaonema
Common name: Chinese evergreen
Light: Moderate light
Care: Keep slightly moist
Tips: Pinch off new leaves to encourage bushiness

Aspidistra eliator
Common name: Cast-iron plant
Light: Low light
Care: Moderate water
Tips: Repot every 3 years to refresh compost

Philodendron xanadu
Common name: None
Light: Moderate light
Care: Allow to dry out between waterings
Tips: Tuck aerial roots back into the pot

Sansevieria trifasciata
Common name: Mother-in-law's tongue
Light: Good light
Care: Low watering requirements
Tips: One of the easiest houseplants to look after! Keep leaves clean

Dracaena marginata
Common name:
Madagascar Dragon tree
Light: Moderate,
indirect light
Care: Moderate water
Tips: Keep well pruned to
control its height

Ficus elastica
Common name:
Rubber plant
Light: Bright to
moderate light
Care: Keep slightly moist;
do not over-water
Tips: Avoid draughts or
cold rooms; keep leaves
clean and shiny

Howea forsteriana
Common name:
Kentia palm
Light: Low light
Care: Keep moist
Tips: Relatively slow-
growing; rarely needs
repotting

Peperomia caperata
Common name:
Emerald ripple
Light: Low to
moderate light
Care: Allow compost to
dry out between waterings
Tips: Over-watering is
about the only thing that
will damage this plant

Epipremnum aureum
Common name:
Devil's ivy
Light: Moderate to
bright light
Care: Moderate water;
tolerates dryness
Tips: Prune twice a year
to keep the plant looking
bushy and full

Spathiphyllum wallisii
Common name: Peace lily
Light: Good light;
tolerates shade
Care: Keep compost
moist; thrives in higher
humidity
Tips: Remove flowering
stems when the blooms
ripen to green; keep leaves
clean and polished

Yucca
Common name: Yucca
Light: Bright to
moderate light
Care: Low watering
requirements – keep dry
Tips: Don't let plants get
too cold

Zamioculcas zamiifolia
Common name:
Fern arum
Light: Low light
Care: Low watering
requirements
Tips: Very tough plant –
can cope with neglect

THE BASICS

LIGHT

The basic building blocks for every plant's survival are light, water and carbon dioxide. Our school biology classes may remind us why they're crucial: a plant 'drinks' water, 'breathes' carbon dioxide and harnesses light to photosynthesize, using the chloroplasts (which give a plant its green colour) in its leaf cells to convert light energy into sugar, or, in other words, plant food. Oxygen is a by-product of this process. If any element is missing, the plant cannot make food and will die.

Although the brightness of light needed by each plant varies, they do all need light to some degree for at least 12 hours a day in the growing season. When deciding which houseplants to have where, take into account not only the amount of light they require but also the light levels in each room. Observe where the light comes in and when, where any shadows form, and how the light moves and changes in intensity during the day. In general, light levels are reduced the closer you are to the ceiling, which is worth noting when choosing plants for cupboard tops or hanging plant displays.

It's said that clean, dust-free windows may raise light levels by as much as ten per cent. Although we haven't tested this scientifically, it's worth bearing in mind.

TIP
The paler the colour of the walls and ceiling, the more natural light is reflected around the room; the opposite is true for dark colours, which absorb light. Be aware of this when you are selecting and positioning plants.

GUIDING LIGHT
This is a rough guide to which light conditions suit which types of plants. To be on the safe side, check the requirements of your chosen plants before you buy.

* **Shade** No plant will survive perpetually low light levels.
* **Semi-shade (hallways & shady spots)** Hardy foliage plants such as *Aspidistra elatior* (cast-iron plant), *Sansevieria trifasciata* (mother-in-law's tongue), *Zamioculcas zamiifolia* (fern arum), compact-growing *Dracaena*.
* **Bright (the average light living room)** Suits nearly all plants. Try palms, flowering plants such as orchids and bulbs, and foliage plants with variegated leaves.
* **Sunlight (bright windowsills)** Choose cacti and succulents, herbs and members of the *Ficus* (fig) family.
* **Full sunlight (windowsills of a south-facing window)** Most houseplants dislike being in direct sunlight, especially in summer, as the sun will 'burn' their leaves.

THE DANGER SIGNS
When there is too little light:
Leaves start to yellow
Variegated leaves turn completely green
Leaves drop
Potting compost stays damp and doesn't dry out as quickly as expected; it may become waterlogged if you continue to water

When there is too much light:
Leaves wilt
Leaves can suffer from brown tips or brown 'scorch' patches
Potting compost dries out too quickly

This page:
Flowering indoor plants, such as the *Cattleya* orchid and the taller *Phalaenopsis* orchids, need plenty of light to ensure they thrive and produce flowers.

This page:
A portable watering can with a long, narrow spout is an essential piece of kit for the indoor gardener.

WHEN & HOW TO WATER

In caring for our houseplants, we are most likely to slip up with the watering. All plants need water to some degree in order to survive. Fact. If a plant dries out, it becomes weak and therefore prone to pests and disease. Ditto if it's too wet. There are no hard-and-fast rules about the frequency of watering – it depends on the plant type, its size and the time of the year, among other things.

For all houseplants, except orchids, carefully and gently pour water into the gap between the plant and the potting compost until the space between the top of the compost and the lip of the container is filled with water – using a small, long-spouted watering can is the easiest way to do this. (Try to avoid getting water on the leaves and flowers, as this can damage them.) Leave to stand for up to ten minutes to allow excess water to drain through the compost. If there is still water sitting on the top, carefully pour it off. There is a difference between keeping the compost moist – which is what most plants want – and wet, which can lead to waterlogging and root rot.

Plants need watering more often in spring and summer in the growing season than in winter. The general rule of thumb is that if the top of the compost looks dry and powdery, you need to water.

TIP
....
It is best to use tepid (room temperature) water. NEVER leave a houseplant standing in water.

HAPPY PLANT HOLIDAYS

It is generally safe to leave your houseplants unattended for up to two weeks. However, if they are left for any longer – especially during the summer growing season – you are taking the risk of plant Armageddon when you return. Failing a friendly plant sitter, there are a few things you can do to avert a disaster:

* Group plants together in a cool spot, away from direct sunlight, to raise the humidity levels around them. Even if you have a plant sitter, grouping your plants together will help them do their job more efficiently.
* Water all your plants thoroughly just before your departure but don't leave them standing in water, such as in a bathtub.
* In winter, leave the heating on – houseplants need a minimum temperature of 15°C (59°F) – ideally, 18–21°C (64–70°F), which is room temperature.
* Watch this space: the development of app-enabled watering systems is underway, which will enable you to water your plants remotely, no matter where you are.

DANGER SIGNS

When there is too much water:
* Young and old leaves fall at the same time
* Leaves develop brown patches
* Plant generally looks a bit mouldy
* Plant develops root rot, with mushy-looking dark roots that can start to smell

When there is too little water:
* Leaf edges turn brown and dry
* Leaves wilt and look limp
* Lower leaves curl and turn yellow
* Leaves may become translucent

PLANT CARE

Indoor plants are surprisingly low maintenance, and with a little regular love and attention, they will thrive. Here's what you need to do and when.

General pointers

All plants need light, water, food and warmth – a bit like people, really – but they vary in the amounts that they need, and that's where you have to do some research. If you treat different types of houseplant in the same way, sooner or later you will run into problems. Broadly speaking, though, there are a few rules that apply to them all.

Generic general-purpose potting compost is fine to use across the board – although there are specialist houseplant mixes available, they're not essential. A liquid feed specifically for houseplants is, however, no bad thing. Use it every couple of weeks during the growing season (mid-spring to early autumn) but never in winter, and make sure you follow the instructions on the packet, as the requirements for different plants will vary. You will also need to reduce the watering of all plants in winter, when they need a rest period, but take care not to let them dry out when you turn on the central heating (see also pages 160–1).

Get into the habit of regularly checking both sides of the leaves and the potting compost for any signs of pests and disease. If you catch any problems at an early stage, you will be able to eradicate them more easily (see pages 166–8).

With the exception of succulents and cacti, all houseplants hate a hot, dry environment, so don't put them near a radiator. Orchids and ferns love the humidity of a bathroom or a kitchen. No plant, however, likes being in a draught.

Avoid stressing your plants by not moving them around too much. Light levels, humidity and temperature can vary a lot from room to room, and a change in these can badly affect a plant.

Pruning

Pruning is not essential for the good maintenance of houseplants. The only reason you would have to prune is if you need to check a plant's growth or if it is becoming a bit misshapen or leggy, which can be an issue with *Ficus* plants.

If pruning is necessary, do it either just at the start or right at the end of the growing season. Also, be gentle on your plant – just prune enough to keep it in shape, and always stop above a bud, no matter how much growth you are removing.

WHAT'S THE PROBLEM?

The reason for plants not looking their best may be easily remedied. For more serious problems, see pages 166–8.

* **Brown leaf tips** Not enough water or too much light
* **Yellow/brown leaves** Insufficient or too much light
* **Flat, brown spots** Too much light or too much water
* **Pale leaves** Too much light or not enough water
* **Drooping leaves** The environment is too dry or too hot
* **Falling leaves** Over- or under-watering or a sudden change in temperature
* **Lopsided growth** The plant is growing towards the light, and the pot is not being turned regularly enough

PETS & HOUSEPLANTS

We all know that some garden plants, such as *Atropa belladonna* (deadly nightshade) and *Digitalis* (foxglove), are poisonous to both people and pets, but, sadly, some of the fabulous houseplants that we have namechecked in this book don't get on so well with our furry friends either. If eaten by your cat or dog, they may cause breathing difficulties, skin and stomach problems, a swollen tongue, vomiting, diarrhoea and, in the worst case, seizures, a coma, even death.

This list of plants that **are not** pet-friendly is by no means comprehensive, so before making any plant purchases, do double-check with your garden centre or veterinarian for compatibility. Remember that it's better to be safe than sorry.

* *Aglaonema modestum* (Chinese evergreen)
* *Aloe vera* (Barbados aloe)
* *Anthurium scherzerianum* (flamingo flower)
* *Asparagus setaceus* (asparagus fern)
* *Begonia rex* (fan plant)
* *Crassula ovata* (money tree)
* *Cyclamen persicum* (Persian cyclamen)
* *Dieffenbachia* (dumb cane)
* *Dracaena fragrans* (corn plant)
* *Epipremnum aureum* (devil's ivy)
* *Euphorbia tirucalli* (finger tree)
* *Fatsia japonica* (Japanese aralia)
* *Ficus* plants, particularly *F. benjamina* (weeping fig)
* *Hedera helix* (English ivy)
* *Hippeastrum* (amaryllis)
* *Hyacinthus* (hyacinth)
* *Monstera deliciosa* (Swiss cheese plant)
* *Narcissus* (daffodil)
* *Philodendron*
* *Sansevieria trifasciata* (mother-in-law's tongue)
* *Schefflera* (umbrella tree)
* *Spathiphyllum wallisii* (peace lily)
* *Tradescantia* (wandering Jew)
* *Yucca elephantipes* (spineless yucca)
* *Zamioculcas zamiifolia* (fern arum)
* *Zantedeschia* (calla lily)

Cleaning

It's true that, if left alone, houseplants will be 'dust gatherers', but this can be prevented. Simply schedule in a few minutes of plant cleaning once a month, along with your watering duties. Cleaning houseplants is actually good for their health – if the leaves get too dusty or dirty, the plant won't be able to photosynthesize properly and so won't thrive.

TOOLS OF THE TRADE

To make caring for your plants as easy as possible, there are a few essential tools.
These are **Ian's personal recommendations:**

* Watering can and mister from Haws
  (hawswateringcans.com)
* Secateurs (pruning shears) from Felco
  (worldoffelco.co.uk) or Burgon & Ball
  (burgonandball.com)
* Hand trowels from Burgon & Ball
  (burgonandball.com)
* Support canes from Harrod Horticultural
  (harrodhorticultural.com)
* Garden twine from Draper
  (drapertools.com)
* Long-handled terrarium trowel and fork
  from Sneeboer (sneeboer.com)

CLEANING NEEDS

Your essential tools for the job are a mister and a damp cloth.

* **Cacti** How you clean a cactus depends on its size and type – and how prickly it is! Small cacti can be very prickly, so run cotton buds (Q-tips) between the spikes to pick up any dust. For large cacti, either fold up a soft cloth and carefully pass it between the thorns, or, better still, put a small sponge or cloth on the end of a stick and use that. A clean, dry paintbrush will also do the trick. Never be tempted to wet a cactus.
* **Ferns & grasses** Regularly misting these plants – which they prefer to watering – cleans them at the same time.
* **Foliage plants** Gently wipe over each leaf with a damp cloth. These plants polish up rather well, so if you want to give the leaves a shine, go back over them with a dry cloth. Don't be tempted to use houseplant polish – a popular pastime in the 1970s – because it can clog the leaf pores.
* **Herbs** A regular misting waters and cleans.
* **Orchids** Gently wipe along the length of their leaves with a damp cloth. The leaves of *Phalaenopsis* (moth orchid) shine up rather well if you go over them afterwards with a dry cloth. Leave the flowers well alone.
* **Palms** These are surprisingly easy to clean. The quickest way is to drape a damp cloth over each palm, place your hands either side of each leaf and gently run the cloths along the length of the leaf from stem to tip.
* **Succulents** Use a clean, dry, soft cloth to run over each leaf gently, from stem to tip.

TIP

Remove dead flowers and leaves the minute you spot them, as these can encourage disease and attract pests.

PLANT DOCTOR

Now you've decided which plants you want to position where, you should know how to keep them healthy. A house isn't a plant's natural environment and, in short, there is no wind or rain to wash away any problems. This puts plants under stress, making them more susceptible to pests and diseases. Although houseplants are primarily affected by pests, these can lead to diseases, such as mould.

Plant stress is usually caused by easily fixed problems: under- or over-watering, too much or too little light, being too hot or too cold, or even being moved about too frequently (see page 163), but there could be more insidious reasons for your plants starting to look less than their best.

Chances are they are suffering from one of the following six common culprits: aphids, mealybugs, scale insects, sciarid flies, spider mites, or whitefly. But if you tackle these quickly, your plants will have a good chance of recovery, so make a habit of checking them regularly.

When treating plants with insecticides, always follow the manufacturer's instructions. Unfortunately, if the pest infestation is severe, you may have to cut your losses and dispose of the infected plant before the problem spreads.

The following gives guidance on how to spot and treat the six most common problems that affect houseplants.

1. Aphids

Appearance Commonly known as greenfly, aphids are tiny flies that also come in pink, yellow or black varieties.

Damage They feed by sucking sap from plants, particularly new tips and leaves, causing stunted growth. The sticky honeydew they deposit can lead to unsightly sooty moulds.

Treatment Use an appropriate insecticide.

2. Mealybugs

Appearance Small, white, spiky insects that slightly resemble maggots and feed on or around the leaves. The females cover themselves and their eggs with a white, sticky material, making them look cottony.

Damage Like aphids, mealybugs excrete honeydew, which can lead to the growth of sooty mould. A serious bout of mealybugs can lead to the plant wilting and the leaves yellowing and dropping.

Treatment Wipe away the mealybugs, as well as the honeydew and sooty mould, with a damp cloth. For a severe infestation, wipe over the affected area with cotton wool or cotton buds (Q-tips) dipped in a solution of methylated spirits (rubbing alcohol) diluted 50/50 with water. Alternatively, spray the insects with an appropriate insecticide.

3. Scale insects

Appearance Flat, brown, hard-shelled insects that cling to the stems or the undersides of leaves.

Damage They suck the sap, weakening the plant, and excrete honeydew, which makes the leaves yellow and sticky. Unsightly sooty mould may then follow.

Treatment Pick off the bugs (yes, we know, yuck!) and then treat with an appropriate insecticide. You will probably have to do this several times over several weeks.

TIP

You can tackle most common pests initially by wiping the affected parts of your plants with a solution of 50/50 water and washing-detergent every five days. If it doesn't seem to be having any effect, you may have to resort to an insecticide.

4. Sciarid flies

Appearance Also called fungus gnats, these tiny black flies with transparent wings can be seen flying around the plant. Their white, opaque larvae have black heads.

Damage The flies are harmless, though annoying and unsightly to have in your home, but the larvae of some species can cause damage by feeding on the plants' new roots.

Treatment Use an appropriate insecticide.

5. Red spider mites

Appearance Tiny, yellowish-green (confusingly!) specks on fine webbing, often found on the undersides of leaves.

Damage A pale mottling effect on the top surface of leaves, which then drop off, is the usual sign of an infestation. This can seriously weaken the plant.

BIOLOGICAL CONTROLS

In his work, Ian uses only biological controls – certain species of insects that prey on problem insects – to treat plant pests because health and safety restrictions prevent the use of pesticides in commercial settings. Biological controls are obviously much better for the environment but they may not be viable in a domestic situation. They tend to be costly and are not usually available in small quantities. Biological controls can also take much longer than standard pesticides to be effective and they aren't brilliant at dealing with a serious bout of anything. Most people are also likely to be squeamish about introducing insects into their homes to treat other insects.

CHECKING OVER THE GOODS

Inspect your plant choices carefully before buying and bringing them home. If they show any signs of insect infestation (see pages 166–8), powdery mildew (fuzzy mould), brown spots, holes or nibbled edges, put them back and seek out healthier specimens.

Treatment Remove infected leaves and spray with an appropriate insecticide – you will have to do this repeatedly because spider mites are persistent. You can also try raising humidity levels by misting the air around the plant or by setting the plant on a tray of gravel filled with water – red spider mites usually attack plants that are already stressed by being in hot, dry air, such as in a centrally heated house.

6. Whitefly

Appearance Tiny, white, moth-like creatures.

Damage The adults excrete sticky honeydew, which can lead to sooty mould, while the larvae suck sap from the plant. An infestation can cause the leaves to turn yellow and fall off. Spreads rapidly.

Treatment Spray with an appropriate insecticide every few days until the flies have been seen off. Only the adult pest is susceptible to insecticides. To treat the larvae, wipe them over with a soapy solution (*see Tip on page 166*) every three to four days until they are eliminated.

TIP

Use the appropriate insecticide for the problem and only spray it on the affected area, avoiding in particular any unaffected new growth or young leaves to prevent damaging them. Always follow the manufacturer's instructions.

SUPPLIERS

Here are some of our favourite nurseries, garden centres, mail order and internet companies and stores for essential equipment, cool containers, home accessories and, of course, plants.

CONTAINERS ET AL

Anthropologie (anthropologie.com). Global, hippy and very cool. Full of colourful, covetable pieces for the home.

Atelier Stella (atelierstella.co.uk). Brighton-based ceramicist who hand-makes the cutest, quirkiest, tripod-legged planters and pots with little faces. These are pots with personality!

B&Q (diy.com). DIY chain, good for essential supplies such as simple terracotta pots, basic tools and a small range of houseplants.

Boskke (boskke.com). Its quirky contemporary hanging planters are great for planting and displaying plants upside down.

C. Best (cbest.co.uk). Huge variety of fabulous containers in pretty much every material, size and style you could think of.

The Conran Shop (conranshop.co.uk). Our go-to for one of the best edits of key pieces in contemporary home design.

Cox & Cox (coxandcox.co.uk). A must if you are after the look that says a little bit rustic, a little bit French, a little bit feminine. Has a strong range of containers for houseplants.

Darkroom (darkroomlondon.com). Co-owners Rhonda and Lulu have fantastic eyes for bold, graphic and, above all, seriously cool interiors objects. Their edited ranges of planters are real statement pieces.

Eleanor Bolton (eleanorbolton.com). This young jewellery designer is almost single-handedly responsible for the revival of hanging macramé plant holders, except hers are brilliantly updated in a range of monochromes and neon brights. Covetable.

Etsy (etsy.com). All about craft, quirkiness, individuality and independence. A great source for unusual planters and containers from small companies and creatives.

Graham & Green (grahamandgreen.co.uk). If it's colourful, unexpected or just plain on-trend, then Graham & Green is the one.

Habitat (habitat.co.uk). A retail stalwart, brilliant at clean-lined and colourful contemporary design. Constantly updates its ranges with must-have pieces. Does a good line in containers, especially in its spring/summer collections.

H&M Home (hm.com). Brilliantly affordable and brilliantly on-trend. Our first call for metallic plant pots, but it's also strong on quick-update home accessories.

Homebase (homebase.co.uk). Stocks all your day-to-day needs from tools to pots, plus a selection of basic houseplants.

IKEA (ikea.com). Affordable, accessible and comprehensive selection of planters, plus the plants to put in them.

Jonathan Adler (uk.jonathanadler.com). American interior designer Jonathan Adler started life as a potter and his range of distinctive, occasionally surreal, vessels and vases is testament to this.

Mia Fleur (miafleur.com). This family-run online store is always a good source for a well-edited range of quirky, hip, statement pieces that are affordable to boot.

Oliver Bonas (oliverbonas.com). Great for affordable, fun and fashionable accessory pieces for the home, from cocktail trolleys to terrariums.

Out There Interiors (outthereinteriors.com). A one-stop online interiors department store – seriously, it has more than 5,000 product lines at any one time, stocking all manner of items, styles and brands, from Art Deco to Scandi.

Rockett St George (rockettstgeorge.co.uk). Cool, contemporary, chic, and with bags of personality, Rockett St George is a must if you are seeking out statement accessories. Jane and Lucy, the co-owners, source high-quality, unusual and desirable home items.

Skandium (skandium.com). A must for keen lovers of Scandi design. Its shops showcase the best of the best from all the Nordic countries, and its range is truly encyclopaedic.

Urban Outfitters (urbanoutfitters.com). Has recently introduced a well-edited range of terrariums, cacti and succulents.

Vitra (vitra.com). Sells beautiful 20th-century design classics as well as new pieces by 21st-century names. Amazing accessories that can be used as unusual planters include the Uten.Silo wall rack, the Toolbox, and Corniches shelves for displaying individual plants.

West Elm (westelm.co.uk). Has a great selection of unusual containers, as well as cool plant stands.

Whichford pottery (whichfordpottery.com). A family-run firm producing a vast range of terracotta pots and planters. Intended for the garden, would look just as good indoors.

PLANTS

Architectural Plants (architecturalplants.com). Set up just over 25 years ago, this is the go-to for bold architectural varieties – think tropical stand-alone statement plants. Mostly garden-focused but does have a selection of palms, yuccas and succulents that would work indoors.

Cactusland at Southfield Nurseries (cactusland.co.uk). The largest collection of cacti in the UK, with around 750 varieties to choose from. Also sells some succulents.

Camden Garden Centre (camdengardencentre.co.uk). Ian's local where everyone's really knowledgeable about plants. A reasonable selection of houseplants, and good for tools.

The Chelsea Gardener (chelseagardener.com). Has an extensive range of indoor plants as well as the pots to plant them in, plus all the tools and equipment needed to care for them.

Clifton Nurseries (clifton.co.uk). Very stylish, selling a lovely range of plants, containers and tools.

Craig House Cacti (craighousecacti.co.uk). Multiple Chelsea Gold Medal winners. Sells both plants and seeds as well as offering plenty of useful care advice.

Dibleys Nurseries (dibleys.com). *The* specialists in *Streptocarpus* (Cape primrose) and winners of multiple

Chelsea Gold medals to show for it. Also stock selected houseplants such as *Begonia rex* (fan plant), *Saintpaulia* (African violet) and *Tradescantia* (wandering Jew).

Every Picture Tells A Story (every-picture.com). This is where to go if you're after a member of the spectacular bromeliad group of plants. Has every variety you could hope for, from *Tillandsia* (air plant) to *Vriesea splendens* (flaming sword).

Hampshire Carnivorous Plants (hantsflytrap.com). Another multiple Chelsea Gold Medal-winning specialist nursery, which sells an extensive range of carnivorous plants.

Indoor Garden Design (indoorgardendesign.com). The business! Has led the way with innovative indoor planting for more than 40 years. Does domestic installations on request.

Interior Landscaping Products (interiorlandscaping.co.uk). Trade supplier of essentials, including planters, feed, tools and watering systems.

Jekka's Herb Farm (jekkasherbfarm.com). Jekka McVicar's herbetum has the largest collection of culinary herbs in the UK and is the source for more unusual varieties.

McBean's Orchids (mcbeansorchids.com). Established in 1879, this orchid nursery lays claim to being the oldest in the UK. Also has one of the most varied selections you will find.

McQueens (mcqueens.co.uk). Cutting-edge contemporary florists. Also has a great range of vessels and will make up a terrarium to order.

Petersham Nurseries (petershamnurseries.com). Expensive but inspiring. Full of beautiful items, from plants to tools.

The Urban Botanist (theurbanbotanist.co.uk). Has a great range of good-value, ready-planted contemporary terrarium designs. Ideal gifts.

TOOLS

Burgon & Ball (burgonandball.com). Has a really well-designed, timeless range of tools.

Felco (worldoffelco.co.uk). Your go-to for every type and variety of secateurs (pruning shears).

Haws (haws.co.uk). Elegant, classic watering cans in every possible shape and size.

Niwaki (niwaki.com). For utterly beautiful gardening tools from Japan. Function and form at its very best.

The Palm Centre (palmcentre.co.uk). Although it's mainly a garden nursery, The Palm Centre also has a brilliant variety of indoor plants, with a particular emphasis on palms and ferns.

Sneeboer (sneeboer.com). Has just launched some terrarium tools to sit alongside its lovely contemporary tool range.

Sophie Conran (sophieconran.com). Has designed a range of lovely tools with Burgon & Ball. Also has a collection of containers.

INDEX

italic page numbers refer to photographs

An Hachette UK Company
www.hachette.co.uk

First published in Great Britain in 2017
by Mitchell Beazley, a division of
Octopus Publishing Group Ltd
Carmelite House
50 Victoria Embankment
London EC4Y 0DZ
www.octopusbooks.co.uk

Publisher: Alison Starling
Editor: Pollyanna Poulter
Creative Director: Jonathan Christie
Designer: The Oak Studio
Senior Production Manager:
Katherine Hockley
Picture Research Manager:
Giulia Hetherington

ISBN 978-1-78472-194-7

PICTURE CREDITS

Key: a above; b below; c centre; l left; r right

123RF Kari Klaustermeier 121bcl; **Alamy** Andrea Jones 95r; D Hurst 107al; Flavia Raddavero/Image Broker 155bcr; John Swithinbank 167ar; Nigel Cattlin 167bl & br; Profimedia.cz 143bl; Steffen Hauser/ botanikfoto 154al; Tashphotography/ Stockimo 79ar; Tim Gainey 79bcr; Vario Images 78ar; Wildlife 130ar; **Camera Press** Flora 79bl; **Dorling Kindersley** 131ar; Sian Irvine 95bcl; Verity Welstead 154br; **Dreamstime.com** Adaychou 131acl; Anna Chelnokova 95bl; Blackslide 95bcr; Dreammasterphotographer 121br; Ileana Marcela Bosogea-Tudor 94al; irabel8 155bl; Joloei 107bl; Karidesign 131al; Kateryna Potrokhova 107ar; Llepet 120bl; Marius Craciun 78br; Nmorozova 154ar; Noppanun Kunjai 155bcr; Panya Chitmedha 107bcl; Sdbower 142ar; Srugina 155bcl; **Fotolia** brhlena 131acr; Dragan Nikolic 143br; Eric Isselée 143bcl; L Bouvier 131bl; Melica

121acr; Morgenstjerne 131bcr; prwstd 131br; vencav 79acl; **GAP Photos** Clive Nichols/ design Clare Matthews 107acr, 143acl, 155ar; Friedrich Strauss 120ar, 130br; Inna Karpova 79bcl; John Glover 95al; Juliette Wade 95acr, 106al, 142bl; Thomas Alamy 143acr, Visions 94ar & bl, 121acl & ar, 130bl, 154bl, 155al; **Garden World Images** Andrea Jones 143ar; Flora Press 94br; Floramedia 78bl, 79br, 121al, 142br, 143al, 155acl; **Getty Images** DEA/C Dani 79acr, G Cigolini 106br; **istockphoto.com** andypantz 167al; Cecilia Möller 120br; **Loupe Images** CICO Books Ltd 142al; **Nature Picture Library** Nick Upton 167cr; **Octopus Publishing Group** Giulia Hetherington 120al; **Science Photo Library** Ron Chapman 107br; **Shutterstock** Amawasri Pakdara 143bcr; Elena Elisseeva 106ar; irabel8 155acr; Kittibowornphatnon 95acl; lynea 121bl; Madlen 95br; Santia 167al; Sergiu Birca 106bl; wasanajai 107acl; **The Garden Collection** Flora Press 131bcl/ Carolinen Bureck 130al, Nova Photo Graphik 78al, 79al.

Pages 10–11: 10al storage tins © Rockett St George; roots glass plant pot 10ac © Nude Living; 10ar succulents © 4th Floor; 10cl Madam Stoltz planters © Out There Interiors; 10cc Bloomingville planters © Out There Interiors; 10cr Lacroix fabric © Designers Guild; 10bl jungle wallpaper © Cole & Son; Nordal planting scheme 10bc © Out There Interiors; 10br Tarovine wallpaper and fabric © House of Hackney; 11al cacti © Darkroom; 11ac restaurant © Rawduck; 11ar terrariums © Rockett St George; 11cl herb vases © Cox & Cox; 11cc look book © Conran; 11cr *Monstera deliciosa* © Habitat; 11bl terrariums © Graham & Green; 11bc cushion © House of Hackney; 11br hanging planters © MiaFleur.

Pages 48–9: All images supplied by Shutterstock apart from 48cc *Monstera deliciosa* © Joy of Plants; 48ar Sunflowers © McQueens; 49bl Vanda Orchids catwalk © Kinder Aggugini, London Fashion Week; 49bc A herb table © James Royall; 49al Paul Smith © Paul Smith.

THANKS & DEDICATIONS

Our thanks to Jean Egbunike, without whom this book would never have come to be.

To the shoot team: Nick Pope, for his unfailing good humour and gorgeous photography; Elkie Brown, for her fabulous styling and boundless energy, and the members of the Indoor Garden Design team, with special thanks to Deanne.

To the owners of all the lovely locations who were kind enough to let us invade their homes and who were so welcoming on the shoot days: Linda, Fintan, Finn and Nansai Mooney; Liliana, Mario, Emilia, Luca and Nico; Joe, Bex, Tilda and Beth; Lindsay, Matt and Olive; Maria, Enzo, Luca, Gabriela and Natalia; Salia and last, but not least, Kally.

The team at Octopus for their commitment to the cause: Alison Starling, Polly Poulter and Jonathan Christie.

From Kara: With love to: Mark, Ailbe and Ned – you are my world; Dad and Cas for their invaluable support during the writing process – both practical and emotional; Mum for her good taste – which, I suspect, got me into interiors in the first place.

From Ian: To my mum, Peggy, and sister, Lisa, for their love and support. Mum, thank you for making that phone call 28 years ago. Also thanks to Allan, for the days and late nights to get this completed and making another dream come true.

KARA O'REILLY

Kara is an experienced and prolific writer and editor of lifestyle and interior design features. She has worked on and contributed to some of the most influential style magazines and newspapers on the market, including *Style* at the *Sunday Times*, *Elle Decoration* and *Livingetc*. Kara is currently Interiors Editor at luxury lifestyle magazine *The Resident*.

IAN DRUMMOND

Ian is Creative Director of Indoor Garden Design. A true north-London boy, Ian uses garden and horticultural design to express his understanding of city living. He has worked on installations for the Barbican Art Gallery and St Pancras Station in London, as well as scooping up an impressive array of medals at the RHS Chelsea Flower Show. Ian's work mainly focuses on creative projects – film premieres, fashion shows and charity functions, including The BAFTAs and the annual Sir Elton John AIDS Foundation's White Tie & Tiara Ball. He is devoted to his craft, and is passionate about bringing the garden into the heart of the home. Ian is also Ambassador of eFIG (European Federation of Interior Landscape Groups) and an RHS committee member.